the WORTH of a SOUL

OTHER BOOKS AND AUDIO BOOKS
BY KRISTEN McKENDRY:

Promise of Spring

The Ties That Bind

Garden Plot

the WORTH *of a* SOUL

From Muslim to Mormon

AYSE HITCHINS *and* KRISTEN McKENDRY

Covenant Communications, Inc.

Printed in the United States of America
First Printing: February 2012

18 17 16 15 14 13 12   10 9 8 7 6 5 4 3 2 1

ISBN-13: 978-1-60861-859-0

To my father
A. H.

To Albert Stumphy,
my teacher, my friend
K. M.

Acknowledgments

I WOULD LIKE TO THANK my husband and my son for sharing this crazy journey with me. Thank you to all those who believed in me when I didn't believe in myself. I sincerely want to thank Pakize Ercan for giving me a home during my ever-challenging university years.

—Ayse

THANK YOU TO SAMANTHA VAN WALRAVEN and all the others at Covenant for their confidence, encouragement, and hard work in bringing this project to print. Thank you to my husband for helping me keep sight of what's important and for giving me the freedom and support to "do my thing." Most of all, thank you to Ayse, Ross, and John for generously allowing me to come along on this latest adventure.

—Kristen

Preface

IT WAS A SIMPLE, ONE-LINE children's song. The brief words conveyed a sweet, profound, but clear gospel message. Surely I could translate it without any difficulty at all. I sat down without preparation, knowing I could whip it out in a few minutes.

But six hours later, crumpled papers cluttered the floor like scattered popcorn balls, the eraser on my pencil was worn to nothing, and I sat staring at the blank page in front of me with a pounding headache and tears of frustration running down my cheeks. I couldn't capture the tone and message of the song. It was like trying to round up soap bubbles—the words eluded me, fell apart, evaporated into nothing. I couldn't find that richness of meaning and still have the words fit the music. What had seemed like a simple little message turned out to have hidden depths I couldn't reach.

"This is ridiculous!" I groaned. "It's only one line! Surely I know my own language well enough to write one line!" But I couldn't do it.

Finally, I took a break and went to the window to look out at the snow. The white world beyond my driveway was as blank as my mind. What was wrong with me? With all my translation experience the last few months, I shouldn't be encountering this problem. I knew I could do this one, simple task. I had confidence in myself—

Ah.

That was what was wrong, of course. I had confidence in myself, but that wasn't where my confidence belonged. I couldn't rely on myself alone to carry me through. This wasn't *my* work. It wasn't *my* translation. I couldn't do it on my own. I knew I needed to repent.

Several prayers later (for both forgiveness and guidance) I was able to sit down at the desk and write out the words, the precise combination to fit the music and the exact meaning of the hymn. It flowed from my pencil onto the page in a warm rush, and I sat back and looked at the perfect results for a long time.

It was a very humbling and eye-opening experience for someone who was naturally very independent. I gained a new understanding that day that this Church project wasn't just about changing English into Turkish. It was about changing *me*.

Section One
Living in Silence

Chapter One

"For in the time of trouble he shall hide me in his pavilion."
—*Psalm 27:5*

NOTHING HAPPENS TO ME GRADUALLY. My life has been a series of events with abrupt beginnings and sudden endings. The first was my birth in a small, impoverished village in southern Turkey, though I didn't learn about that until I was much older. I thought I was from the great city of Istanbul, the only daughter of a wealthy chemical engineer.

But no. I suppose, in truth, my story really begins earlier than that, with the birth of another child, a girl named Turkan.

At the time of Turkan's birth, her mother was a young, unmarried girl, a catastrophe in Muslim Turkey. The father, a prominent man in society, refused to marry her to cover her shame. The young mother went to court to try to force the man to take responsibility. When he still refused, the mother declared, "If you don't want the child, neither do I."

So there they were, two furious people facing each other over an unwanted six-month-old baby. Clearly someone had to take the child. It so happened that the judge of the court and his wife had wanted a baby, and here was one who needed a home. The judge wrapped Turkan up, took her home, and raised her as his own.

Perhaps it was the abrupt change in her own early life. Perhaps it was genetics inherited from her reluctant parents. Perhaps it was growing up knowing that the people who should have loved her most wanted her least. I didn't analyze the cause as I grew up—I wasn't aware of her history then. I only knew that Turkan, the woman I called *Mother*, was a fierce and frantic flame who either tempered or scorched but never warmed.

* * *

The bright sun shone down on the street, turning the white stone of the buildings to apricot. A breeze saved us from the heat, bringing with it the smell of the sea and also good cooking coming through the neighbors' windows. I wore a nice dress for our walk—peach, with a matching ribbon. We were spending the day together, one of Dad's rare days off. We were treating it like a holiday. Dad stopped at the market and bought me candy, sticky and red like rubies in the sun, and I was very careful not to let it touch my dress. At the market, I saw a woman who lived in our building, and I was pleased to have her see me with my pretty dress, walking with my tall and handsome father. Well, I suppose he wasn't that tall, really, but that he was handsome could never be in doubt. With his unusual blue eyes, strong, smooth-shaven jaw, and lean build, he was a striking figure, striding through the market with the sunlight on his chocolate hair. I was very happy. We talked, he and I, as if we were two adults walking along together.

It was 1969, and I was probably around six years old. My age has always been a slippery thing. Throughout my life it has been an elusive thread running through every event and memory like one off-key note in a chord. Ask any North American two-year-old how old she is and she will cheerfully hold up two fingers. I could never answer that simple question. Back then, the Turkish didn't bother much with paperwork or registering births, so I didn't know the exact year of my birth. But I was just tall enough for Dad to take off his hat and hold it over my head like a shade, his wrist resting lightly on my dark hair, just the right height for him to lean on.

As we climbed to the higher streets, we could see the blue wedge of sea and the spreading red roofs and white stone of Istanbul. The colors of the city always made me think of good food—lemon, vanilla nougat, butter, cream. There were many trees throughout the city, but the Blue Mosque's six pointed minarets dominated the skyline. I didn't know why it was called the Blue Mosque, since it was white on the outside, but maybe it had something to do with the tiled interior I had never seen. I thought its stacked domes looked like a cake. Even though I was never allowed into the streets by myself, I was confident that if I ever got lost, I would be able to find my way home again by orienting myself to those minarets.

As the sun's fierceness faded, my short legs began to tire. My stomach started to wonder what supper might be. But we kept walking, and because it was magical to be away from the gloom of the apartment and to have Dad all to myself for an entire day, I didn't mention my weariness.

Toward the end of the day, we turned back at last, but we didn't turn down the right street. Instead, Dad kept walking and then stopped in front of a villa about ten minutes from our apartment. It was a solid-looking building made of honey-colored stone, and there was a great iron door in front. Dad sat down on a large rock by the gate, and I thought he must need to rest. If he were tired, why hadn't he turned down our road toward home?

Dad set aside his hat. His face grew solemn. He took my small hands in his and drew me against his knees.

"Ayse," he said. I always liked how he said my name, "*Eye*-shuh," like a soft sneeze. It made it sound cheerful.

"Yes?" I thought maybe he had another present for me.

"I'm going to go home now," he said gently. "I'm going to leave you here."

"What do you mean?" I asked, wondering if he were teasing. I didn't know this game. "What about me?"

"This is your new place," Dad said. "It is a school. You are old enough to go to school now."

I knew the other children in our apartment building, older than I, went to school. I saw them walking to school in the mornings and coming home again in the evenings with their sweaters and leather bags. I had always wanted to be one of them, to wear a tidy new uniform and carry a bag of books to school. But I didn't understand what he was saying about this honey-colored building.

"You are going to stay here, and I will come see you when I can."

"But I'll come home to you and Mother tonight," I said firmly.

"No. At this school, the students live here and only come home to visit sometimes."

It felt as if cold water were being poured over my head, down my back. I gripped his hands with alarm. "I want to go with you!" I cried.

"Not this time, little one. We can't go together," he said, and I saw him begin to cry. That alarmed me more because my dad never cried.

It was as if the earth had split in half under my feet. If Dad was crying, the whole world had gone wrong.

"Why can't I go home with you?" I asked, tears blurring my own eyes. "Why can't I go to the day school?"

"Home isn't a good place for you," Dad told me. "I want you to be safe and happy. You need to stay here."

His voice was gentle, but his words chilled me. *Safe and happy*. But I only felt that way when I was with him.

"Can I come home tomorrow?" I begged.

"No, I'm sorry. You are going to live here for a while, Ayse."

I knew our apartment was only ten minutes away. I knew I could run there, even tired as I was. Surely he didn't mean to leave me and walk home alone. The sun was going down. I began to panic.

I grabbed his coat and clung to it frantically, crying openly now but silently. I always cried silently. I had learned very early not to attract attention to myself.

"I don't want to be alone," I wailed.

"You're not going to be alone," Dad said. "You're going to have friends and teachers, people to take care of you. You will like it one day."

I heard a noise behind me and turned to see a man walking toward us from the open gate. He was plump and had a friendly face, with graying hair and olive skin. I pressed myself against my father's legs, but Dad stood and pushed me slightly from him as the man approached.

"This is the principal," Dad told me. "He is in charge of this school."

The man shook my father's hand. "Mr. Necmi Gencata?" he said, and my dad nodded in greeting.

Then the principal stooped to my level and took my hands in his as my dad had done. His hands were foreign and hot. I wanted to pull away but was afraid of what he would do if I did.

"Hello, Ayse. We are happy to have you join us," he said, and his voice was deep and kind. "You mustn't cry. You are a big girl now, and you are going to be fine."

It dawned on me with horrible clarity that this had all been planned ahead of time. This man knew my name, knew I was coming. My beloved father had *planned* to leave me here. He'd known it all day long as we'd walked the streets together, as he'd bought me treats. I was stunned. Didn't he *want* me to live with him anymore? This had to be some terrible mistake. Did Mother know what he'd planned? She hadn't indicated so this morning. She'd only muttered a vague, distracted good-bye as we'd left the apartment. What would she do when I didn't come home?

Before I knew what was happening, the man pulled me from my father and through the gate. The big white iron door closed, blocking my view of Dad, who stood there in the street waving and still crying. The door closing made an awful sound, a hollow boom and clang that shook my bones. I remember that sound even now. I cried and cried and cried. To this day, I can't live behind closed doors; all doors in my house are open.

Chapter Two

"For thou hast been my defence and refuge in the day of my trouble."
—*Psalm 59:16*

I WAS AT THE BOARDING school for five years.

The private school was a small villa, formerly a residence, in the wealthy neighborhood of Istanbul called *Levent*, which has since become the high-rise business district of the city. The school was not a large one, with only about twenty-four students, and once I grew used to it, it was actually very nice. The white walls seemed to make the rooms appear bigger than they were, and the vinyl and cement floors were cool even in the summer. There was always a subdued quiet, like in a library. The school had a beautiful, big garden in a walled area of the grounds where tall grass and flowers grew. I loved the daisies. It was heavenly to sit under the trees and make a tiara out of fresh daisies. Behind the school, there were orchards of fruit trees, and it became a favorite pastime of mine to sit and watch the sunlight filter through the green, gray, and yellow of the leaves. It was a peaceful garden.

But I didn't know all of that my first night there. I only knew my beloved father had left me with strangers. The principal took me through the hushed hallways, past many closed doors. His stride was longer than my dad's, and I had to scurry to keep up.

We stopped at last in the open doorway of a small room. The room had one small window and three sets of three-tier bunk beds stacked in it. I was told to choose the one I wanted. I wiped my eyes and looked at those nine beds in wonder. I'd never seen such a thing, and I was shocked at the thought of nine people sleeping in one room all together. Who were the other eight? At home we each had a room to ourselves. I didn't belong here.

"It's all right, Ayse," the principal said kindly, putting his hand on my dark hair. "You choose the one you want."

I saw a little tiny wooden ladder leading up to each top bunk. I chose one of the very top ones. It appealed to me that you could go up and down that little ladder, as if it were a fort or a tree house.

And then I noticed a small bag in the corner of the room, a bag I recognized. I went to it and saw it held some of my clothes and things. I supposed my father must have left it there in advance because I didn't remember him carrying anything with him that day. The bag was small, the belongings few—I guess at that age, I didn't need much anyway— but it was good to see something familiar.

"The other children are about to have their dinner," the principal told me. "Come with me, and I will make sure you get something to eat."

I wasn't sure I could eat; I felt sick to my stomach. But I followed him as directed.

The eating hall was larger than the other rooms, with a high ceiling held up by great wooden beams. The children all ate at one big table, on which were placed water jugs, glasses, and cutlery. I was intimidated, looking at all those unfamiliar faces that turned toward us as we entered. The children all looked to be about my age or a little older.

The principal showed me how to pick up a metal, compartmentalized food tray and line up to get food from the kitchen staff. I hardly paid any attention to what was served onto the tray. I was terrified I would drop it in front of everyone and spill everything, but I managed to carry it to the table without incident. I took the chair I was given and tried not to look at anyone else, in spite of my curiosity. The room was surprisingly quiet, with only the occasional clink of utensils. There was no whispering or squirming or swinging of legs. I eventually learned that when the teachers were present, the students were disciplined and quiet. They were only noisy at recess, when they let all their energy out in the courtyard.

To my surprise, the principal and teachers ate with us at the big table. The principal sat beside me, and in spite of my misery, I felt a glimmer of comfort. With him beside me, I felt a little like a grown-up at a dinner party.

Eventually, I would come to love mealtime. We gathered together many times a day, but of all the gatherings, mealtimes were the most special. The pleasant smell of frying food would fill the house, which always made me feel comfortable. We could set aside the whole world for an hour and enjoy delicious meals together as friends, like I imagined a big, happy family would do. I could pretend briefly that the other children were my siblings. Even today, when I smell a hot dog and fries, my mind goes back to that school.

* * *

That evening, we children were taken to our bedrooms, nine children in each. I felt almost as if we were sheep in a storybook, shuffling down the hall in a herd, a small group being separated off through each door we passed, funneled into our separate stalls. My bag held a nightgown, and I changed quickly with the other girls, self-conscious at changing in front of them, though no one paid any attention to me. I found the bunk I had chosen earlier and climbed into it. I was glad there was a metal rail to keep me from falling off because the floor looked a very long way down. I lay there with the blanket pulled up to my chin, feeling like a bird high up in a nest, and watched the other girls slot themselves into their bunks without any chatter or laughter. The night teacher, a tall, stern-looking woman, turned off the bedroom light and said, "Go to sleep. I don't want to hear a peep out of you."

When you're little and lost, you just do what you're told to do. I lay in that unfamiliar bed, looking up at the ceiling in the dark, so close above me. I wasn't used to having the ceiling so close; it was oppressive. I could hear the other children in the room, all unknown to me, breathing quietly. Someone coughed. It was hot, and the sheets were stiff and unfamiliar. I knew that not ten minutes away, my father lay in his bed, and in the room next to his, my own bed lay empty. I began crying silently, the corner of the sheet stuffed into my mouth, terrified that the other children might hear me.

I must have fallen asleep at some point, worn down by shock and fear. In the morning, I was jerked awake when a woman opened our door, snapped on the lights, and called, "Good morning! Time to wake up." She went out again, and I huddled and watched as the other children climbed out of bed and began to dress. The sunlight was weak in the window, and I knew it was very early. One of the girls noticed I wasn't moving and climbed up to give me a poke with her finger.

"You have to get up," she ordered. "Hurry!"

Her voice held a note of panic, and I fumbled my way awkwardly down the ladder in alarm. Clearly something terrible was about to happen. I found my dress and yanked it on, just as the woman returned. She noticed right away that my bed was unmade.

"Who sleeps here?" she demanded.

I considered my options and decided I'd better respond before someone told on me. I slowly raised my hand.

The woman eyed me a moment. She must have realized I was new because her voice was more gentle as she explained, "Here, we make our beds every morning."

I couldn't see how I could make the bed when it was three tiers up. I was too small to reach it from the floor. The ladder only reached the near corner, and my arms were short like the rest of me. I would have to climb up on the bed itself.

"But how am I . . . to pull the blankets up when I have to . . . kneel on them?" I stammered.

"I'll show her," offered one of the girls. She was one of the older ones and much taller than I. She had short dark hair like mine, and her smile was kind. I watched her climb up the ladder and make my bed. She knelt on the mattress to tuck in the blankets on the far side, against the wall, giving little jumps to free the blankets from her weight. Then she stood on the ladder to finish tucking in the front side, tightly so there were no wrinkles. I was shorter than she, and I wasn't sure I could learn to do it myself, but I gave her a grateful smile when she returned to the floor. Maybe if I were very nice to her, she would do it for me every morning. Maybe, just maybe, she would be my friend.

Satisfied, the teacher led us in a line down the hall to the dining room for breakfast. I fell into step with the girl who had made my bed, and I watched carefully whatever she did. I made sure to imitate her so I did nothing wrong while I tried to figure out this new place.

At home, I had learned to be as silent as possible, trying to be unnoticed, living under the radar. But over the next couple of days, I watched the other children at the school, and it seemed to me that the noisiest ones received the most attention from the teachers. Those who volunteered answers in class were given better treatment than those who had to be called upon. Those who spoke up in protest when things didn't go their way seemed to get results. Even the ones who spoke up at dinner seemed to get bigger portions of food than the others. The quiet ones, like me, were often overlooked. I had never been a troublemaker or one to whine or complain. At home, my dad had known pretty well what I wanted or needed without my having to say anything. But I began to sense that if I wanted anything at this school, I was going to need to learn to speak up. I was going to need to learn to cry out loud.

After a week or so, I had the opportunity to try it myself. One of the girls in my class had taken to pinching or shoving me when the teacher wasn't looking. When we stood in line, she pushed in front of me. She knew I wouldn't say anything. But one day, when she pushed me out of the way so she could get a better look at something the teacher was showing us, I gathered my courage and called out, "Stop that!"

The room went silent, and the teacher glared at me. I pointed at the other girl.

"She shoved me."

The girl looked astonished and started to deny it. But the teacher told her firmly to move over and make room for me. To my surprise, the girl obeyed. After that, she didn't bother me anymore because she knew I might shout and get her into trouble.

After a few experiments with this, I learned to raise my voice consistently. If you were not silent, people took better care of you.

I already knew how to read and write when I started school. Dad had always read with me as I was growing up, classics and fairy tales, history and science, and even bits about current events from the newspaper. I knew Dad was a highly learned individual and had several degrees, and he had often told me how much he loved education. It had set him apart from our neighbors, who had not received as much schooling and held jobs that, I gathered, were not as lofty. Being able to read and write made it easier for me when I entered the school. It meant fewer new things to have to grapple with all at once. When all else was unfamiliar, books were old friends I could gravitate to. In fact, for those first few miserable weeks, books were my only friends and comfort. Sometimes I would even smuggle them into bed with me and sleep clutching them to me like stuffed animals.

It got easier with time and as I got to know the other children. They were generally friendly, but none of them really stood out among the others. We didn't have a lot of free time, so there wasn't much opportunity to play, but we got to know each other between classes and in the evenings.

One day at recess, one of the girls who was a few years older than I was asked me what my parents did.

"My father is a chemical engineer," I told her a bit proudly. I knew this had always gotten a good reception from other people when my father told them what he did, and I was pleased to see the other children's faces look suitably impressed.

"And what about your mother?" the girl asked.

"She doesn't have a job. She stays home," I said.

"Then why are you here?"

I blinked at her, not sure what she meant. "To learn," I said slowly.

"No, I mean, why do you go to a boarding school? Why not go to the day school and live at home if your mother is there?"

I wasn't sure how to answer this, so I shrugged and said, "This place is all right. My father wanted me to come here."

"Well, my father is a businessman, and he is always away on trips all over the world," she told me. It was my turn to look impressed. "And my mother is a flight attendant," she went on, "so I have to go to boarding school. There's no one at home to take care of me."

"Me too," another girl confided. "My parents are always traveling, so I had to come here."

"Didn't you want to come to this school?" I asked.

"Are you crazy? I wanted to go to the day school."

"Me too," chimed in another girl who was listening in.

"Sometimes I think this school is just a holding tank," declared the first girl. "They're just entertaining us until our parents come home."

The others nodded. I wasn't sure what a holding tank was, but I said nothing. It was clear though that these other children were much like me—away from home and family against their will. With that realization came the thought that perhaps we could become friends.

The first visiting day, Dad came to see me. I wasn't sure what I expected. I thought perhaps since my world had changed so much, he would have changed too. I had the vague idea that perhaps I would be angry with him, resentful that he had left me so abruptly, and I was worried about this. I genuinely didn't want to be angry with him because we had always been such close friends. I didn't want that to change.

But when I entered the visiting room, there he was, the same old, wonderful Dad, the same handsome face, the same gentleness, and the same love in his blue eyes. I ran to him and threw my arms around his neck, and all was right again. My worries had been groundless. He sat beside me and talked to me as he always had, about news and things going on in the city and about our neighbors. I soaked up the sound of his voice like rain on dry earth. He had brought small goodies in his pockets to surprise me with, and he kept patting my hand or putting his arm around my shoulders as if he couldn't believe I were real and had to keep reassuring himself that I was there.

But our time together was too short. And the whole time he was there, I could only think of one thing: that he could go away again at the end of the day and I couldn't. He would go out through that big iron door, and I would have to stay behind. It was almost as painful as the first day that door had clanged shut between us. Dad came to see me every chance he got, but I missed him terribly between visits.

My mother never came to visit.

As I grew older, I realized, of course, that was why I was at the boarding school and not at the day school. Dad wanted me at home with him. But he didn't want me at home with *her*.

* * *

One visiting day after my father had just left, one of my teachers came to me. She was a short, round woman with critical eyes and a permanent frown on her face. She could have been pretty if not for that frown, and there were times I was tempted to tell her so.

"Ayse, where is your father from?" she asked.

"Istanbul," I answered.

"He doesn't look Turkish. He's tall and fair and those suits he wears—well, he looks more Eastern European."

"That's because his father was from Bulgaria," I told her readily. "Before Turkey became a republic, it was part of the Ottoman Empire, and Bulgaria was part of the Empire too. But his father, my grandfather, emigrated here, and Dad was born in Turkey."

The teacher stared at me a moment, and then she said, "How do you know about the Ottoman Empire, child? You haven't studied that part of history yet."

"My father told me about it," I replied.

"He teaches you history?"

"Yes. He told me all about how Turkey became a country. And he taught me that Istanbul used to be called Constantinople and that it was an important center for early Christianity. You know, the Catholic church."

She blinked at this. "Is—is your father Catholic?"

"No. But he reads about things and tells me."

"Is he Muslim, then?"

"He is a spiritual man," I said, echoing back something I had once heard him say to another man. "But he isn't formally religious. My mother is, but she doesn't always cover her head. I don't have to cover mine; it's up to me to choose when I'm older."

The teacher arched an eyebrow. "Did your father tell you that too?"

"Yes. He talks to me about a lot of things."

"Apparently so," she said and turned away, but I noticed on the next visiting day that she kept glancing over at my father and me.

Chapter Three

"My soul is among lions: and I lie even among them that are set on fire."
—*Psalm 57:4*

THE FIRST SUMMER AFTER I entered the school, I was allowed to go home on break. I could hardly wait. I was eager to see my old room again, be among my things, play with my long-lost toys, and sleep in my old bed without the oppressive ceiling leering above my face. Above all, I was overjoyed at the thought of being able to see Dad every day and not just on visiting days. I packed my small bag with the things I would need over the summer, and I said good-bye to my friends, promising to tell them all about my vacation when I returned in the fall.

As we waited in the visiting room for our parents to come for us, we chatted excitedly about what we were looking forward to the most. None of us even wanted to think about having to come back when summer was over.

"I'll see my baby sisters again," said one girl. I remember her saying this because I always felt sorry that I didn't have any younger brothers or sisters. I knew this girl had three little sisters, and it seemed unfair to me that she should have so many when I had none. I had an older brother named Omer Toksoz, but he was much older than I and was in and out of the house, and we were not close.

"I miss my mother's cooking," another girl sighed. "I am so tired of bulgar."

"Oh yes, my mother is a wonderful cook," cried another girl.

"In my family, my father does all the cooking," I said proudly.

They all looked at me in disbelief.

"Your father cooks?"

"Yes, he makes great things to eat," I said. My stomach was already growling. I knew he would have made something special for that evening, my first night home. Kebabs, maybe, and rich, nutty *baklava*, sticky with orange-blossom syrup.

"My father can't boil water," someone whispered.

"I don't know if mine can," declared another. "I've never seen him try." They all laughed.

"Does he clean the house too?" someone joked.

"Yes, of course. He does all the housework," I replied with a shrug.

The looks they gave me sobered me. I felt a funny hollowness in my stomach that I didn't understand, and my cheeks felt hot.

"Why?" I asked. "Don't your fathers clean the house?"

"That's women's work," my friends said, and I heard scorn in their voices.

* * *

When Dad came at last, I could hardly contain my joy. There were two whole months ahead of me with no school, no teachers, no crowded classrooms, and a bedroom all to myself. Dad carried my little bag, and I skipped beside him. Our apartment building was just ten minutes away, but in that short walk, I felt like I was returning to another world. Our street was familiar, tree-lined and wide, sloping slightly downhill. The smells were familiar: the blossoms on the trees, the window boxes with early flowers, the good scent as people started to prepare their dinners. The air tasted of spring. The slice of sea I could see beyond the rooftops was the color of peaches, lit by the cheerful, orange setting sun.

The doorman in the lobby greeted me politely as if I were a grown-up returning from a business trip, which made me feel taller, but I was embarrassed to realize I had forgotten the man's name. Had I been gone that long? My father nodded hello and exchanged a friendly greeting with him, but he didn't say the man's name, so I just nodded in greeting too and said nothing.

We went up the stairs and along the carpeted hallway. Dad pushed the door of our apartment open and ushered me inside as if I were a guest.

"Welcome home, my dear," he said, and his face was so happy I wanted to cry.

Our apartment was just as I remembered it. Delightedly, I went into the living room, looking around, feeling I needed to reacquaint myself with everything at once. I touched the carved wood of the table and the smooth, cool walls, felt the carpets beneath my feet, and smelled the familiar, warm smells of home.

Mother was sitting on a chair near the window, looking out. She wore a dark, expensive-looking dress and had a navy scarf tied over her dark hair. As always, there were several handkerchiefs of different colors tied at her waist. She hadn't moved when I'd entered, and it actually took me a moment to realize she was there. It was as if she were a shadow, part of the furniture.

"Mother!" I called.

She turned her head, but she didn't rise. Her round face didn't smile. She looked at me silently for a long moment. Then she looked out the window again, at the people walking by in the courtyard below.

I stood rooted to the carpet, my joy dampened as suddenly and as surely as if she'd spat on me. The old queasiness filled my stomach, making me realize suddenly that I hadn't felt it for several months. I hadn't noticed before. How could I have forgotten that feeling? I felt stupid just standing there. I could feel Dad's eyes on me. I kept my chin up as if nothing were wrong, turned, and went to my bedroom.

My room had been kept exactly the way I'd left it so suddenly all those months ago. There were my shelves of toys, my books, the closet doors half open to show all the clothes I'd forgotten I owned. I threw myself on my stomach across the bed and pressed my face into the blankets, soaking in the smell of home. Dad set my bag beside my bed and told me to wash up because dinner would be ready soon. He was smiling as he left the room.

I could smell meat roasting, and my mouth watered with anticipation. I bounced up and went to wash. But once I was seated at the table, it was difficult to eat. I glanced at Mother, sitting in the chair Dad had pulled close to the table. She ate with all her attention on her plate, and I wondered if she even tasted the food Dad had prepared. There was no indication on her face of what she thought of her meal—or of my return. She always had impeccable table manners. She didn't look up through the entire meal.

Dad talked constantly as we ate, as if trying to fill the space my mother's silence made. I did my best to respond, and I told him about my studies and my friends as if he hadn't seen me every weekly visiting day since I'd gone away. Between us, we managed to carry the conversation through dinner. I didn't ask where Omer was; all my life, my older brother had come and gone as he pleased, and I was used to him being away more than he was home. I knew better than to bring him up because I wanted tonight to go smoothly, and talking about Omer would only upset my parents. They fought over Omer a great deal because they had differing ideas on how to raise him.

I helped wash the dishes after dinner, and Mother silently returned to her seat by the window, her hands plucking at each other in her lap. Dad and I listened to the news on the radio for a while, and then he turned on some classical music. I felt a lot more cheerful listening to that music with its soaring strings and stirring tympani. I finally felt I was at home. The music soothed me and made the ache in my stomach lessen.

I had made a card at school for Mother, and now I took it from my bag and carried it to her. Holding it out to her, I said, "All the girls made something for their mothers. It's a poem."

Mother looked at it a moment, and then she selected one of the handkerchiefs in her lap, a sky-blue one. She always used handkerchiefs to handle things that came from outside the apartment. Only Mother knew the order and which handkerchief was to be used for which purpose. Holding it around her fingers like a glove, she took the card from me and looked at it. I didn't think she looked at it long enough to read the poem though.

"Very nice," she murmured and handed it back to me.

I didn't know what to do with it. Should I put it back in my bag? Go put it in her room? I stood awkwardly, fighting tears I refused to let fall. But Dad rescued me, reaching down to take it from my hand and holding it up to examine it carefully, as if he were appraising great art.

"It's a beautiful poem, Ayse," he told me. "I know you made this for your mother, but is it all right if I take it to my office and keep it on my desk? I would like to be able to read it every day. It will be a special reminder of you."

I immediately felt much better. Even at that young age, I recognized what my father was doing, and I loved him all the more for it.

When it was bedtime, I hesitated and then went to stand at Mother's knees.

"Good night, Mother," I said and waited.

After a moment, her eyes slid to me, and a light came into them as if she were just now recognizing me. "Good night, Ayse," she said and smiled. She softly patted me on the hand, like the brush of a cat's whiskers. By the time I reached my bedroom door, she had already returned to the view of the now empty courtyard.

* * *

I lay in bed in my big, empty room, thinking, staring up at the ceiling that now seemed so far above me in the dark. I had always known Mother was different from other mothers, but it was more obvious to me now that I had been away for a few months. I had seen my friends' mothers come to visit them at the school, smiling and gentle and cheerful women. They had brought surprises and hugged their daughters and laughed. They had asked questions about their daughters' classes and the friends they'd made. They'd exclaimed in delight over the little gifts their daughters had made them. They hadn't acted as if their daughters weren't even in the room. They hadn't used handkerchiefs to touch objects, one color for keys, one color for doorknobs, one color for books. And sky blue, apparently, for poetry.

Dad had to leave very early the next morning for work, taking three buses to reach the factory where he was in charge of fabric dyes. I knew the routine; for the most part, I kept to my room, where I got reacquainted with all the books and toys I had missed over the past few months. I ventured out only to have lunch, a simple green salad and sandwiches Dad had prepared before he left. Mother had her head covered today with a dark green scarf edged with fine beading. No matter what, Mother always dressed well and took pride in her appearance. When Dad wasn't home, she didn't seem to know what to do with herself. She paced from window to door to bookshelf to window again. What little she said didn't seem to be directed at me but instead at the furniture, the floor, or the people walking past below the window. Her eyes wouldn't land on me but darted sideways and away, as if she were trying to watch invisible dragonflies. She ate standing, rocking on her feet, and only settled down when I turned on some music for her.

When I couldn't stand to watch Mother anymore, I let myself out of the apartment and walked down the stairs to the yard. In my life before boarding school, I sometimes went to a neighbor's home while Dad was at work, but usually I preferred to just play by myself. There was green space in front of and behind our building, with a scattering of trees and thickly filled flowerbeds. I especially loved the great big willow tree in the backyard. I went to it now and crawled under the curtain of slender, hanging branches to sit on the cool grass with my back against the rough trunk. It was the perfect spot to muse and dream. With the fronds nearly touching the ground around me, it felt as if I were in my own little house, sheltered and hidden. Pieces of bark and bits of flowers served as plates and food. A discarded bottle top I'd found in the street sufficed for a tiny teacup. I spent the rest of the day quite happily lost in my own imagination—an imagination that was well developed because I'd spent so much time alone as a child. Mother never played with me, and Dad was at work most of the time.

I waited until evening began to fall and men began to gather around the gambling tables set in the courtyard, and then I went back to the apartment. Mother was in her chair at the window. I went to my room and waited for Dad to finish his ten-hour shift and come home.

He arrived at last, filling the apartment with his welcome. I could feel a tangible sense of relief when he came in. He had a big smile and hug for me and a gentle touch on the shoulder for Mother. He cooked us supper, and then he and I went out for a brief walk around the neighborhood. It couldn't be a long walk because it was growing dark and he had a lot to do back at the apartment, but it was a joy to me to be with him again as we had always been, walking along together and talking. Our last walk had been the day he'd left me at the school, and I was happy to have a new, different walk to erase that one in my mind.

Tomorrow, he said, was the beginning of his vacation time, and he was going to take me to the park.

When we returned home, Omer was there. He hadn't changed at all—handsome, stylish, wearing the latest clothes. He tweaked my ear, ruffled my hair, and said I was looking taller. Dad didn't look too pleased to see him.

Mother was seated at the table going through her gold coins. She had a habit in the evenings of counting the gold in which she had invested. I sat and watched her for a while as she went carefully through the little stacks. I liked the clinking sound they made and the way they caught the light. When she finished counting, Mother returned the coins to the little plastic pill bottles in which she kept them. Then she wrapped the bottles in a sock and wrapped the sock in a pillowcase. This she rolled up and tucked into the beautiful black-walnut wardrobe in her room. It was always the same ritual, and watching her was somehow comforting to me. She seemed calm and content when she was counting her coins.

At the beginning of every month, Dad would bring home his salary, in cash, and place it in an envelope in Mother's wardrobe. The next morning, Mother would get up, find it, and say, "Oh, look what the angels have brought us." She really truly believed angels were helping us financially.

Dad would just shake his head and say with a funny half smile, "I don't think she will ever understand that I'm working."

Dad and Omer discussed politics often, that being the only subject they really shared an interest in. A Marxist, Omer was very bright and had read a lot of books on the topic. I wasn't very clear what Marxism was, but I knew it was something he and Dad felt very strongly about, and their discussions could grow quite heated. They both believed in Communism but had different approaches to it. I understood even at that young age that my father felt each person should work for the good of society, while Omer felt the society should work for each person. Tonight when Omer said something about the value of labor, Dad raised his voice. "What do you know about labor?" he barked. "You haven't worked a day in your life."

"Why should I?" Omer replied with a laugh. "I have everything I want."

"Yes, you do, only because Turkan can't say no to you!"

Omer frowned at this, and I could tell he wanted to turn it into an argument, but Dad stood abruptly and said it was time for bed. Mother rose and retired to her bedroom without a word, but Omer took his jacket and left the apartment, slamming the door behind him. Young as I was, I knew he was going out to drink and that he would likely not be home again for a day or two. I kissed Dad on the cheek and went to my own room.

I lay awake in bed long into the night and listened to my father cleaning in the living room. He was trying to move quietly, but once in a while he forgot himself and started humming, and I smiled at the sound.

It was nearly midnight before he finished folding the laundry and I heard the door of his room close.

The next day Dad took me to the park, and it was how it had been before, just he and I spending time together, being happy. It was much better than sitting in the visiting room with him at school. Now that the tension of the night before had dissipated, I was able to ask him to explain what Marxism was, and he did so, trying to put it into easy terms I could understand. I didn't get it all, but I loved the sound of his patient voice and made encouraging noises to keep him talking. I tried to make my responses intelligent, but I don't think it mattered much to Dad what I said. He enjoyed our time together as much as I did, no matter what topic we were discussing.

"There is always so much to learn, Ayse," he told me. "You can spend your whole life learning new things and never grasp it all. Your life will always be fulfilling and interesting so long as you keep learning."

I promised I would, though it didn't seem to me that I had much choice in the matter. From my perspective, I would be in school the rest of my life.

"And you must use what you learn wisely," Dad added. "It doesn't help you if you know something and don't use it well." He paused then went on. "You mustn't pay much attention to the things Omer says and does. He is into things he shouldn't be, things that will only bring him grief. If he would only get a steady job, I would worry less about him. He is an example of someone who has learned a lot but still knows very little."

I found it easier to breathe when we were away from the apartment, and I was reluctant to return. But there was dinner to prepare and cleaning to do, so we finally returned home. When we arrived, I was surprised to see Omer sitting at a table in the courtyard below our apartment playing cards with some of his friends. I knew he gambled a lot; that was another one of the things he and Dad fought about frequently. When he saw us approaching, Omer leaned back lazily, put a cigarette to his lips, and flicked his lighter. But instead of lighting his cigarette, he lit a piece of rolled-up paper and used that to light his cigarette. When we got closer, I saw that the paper was an American ten dollar bill. He waved it around to put out the flame, gave his friends a wide grin, and they laughed. Omer was wearing a blue velvet jacket, and with his cleanly cut hair and suave posture, I thought him very handsome. Dad didn't look impressed.

"This is what you consider a good, productive way to live?" he asked grimly. "Where do you get the money for all this gambling?"

"I win it," Omer replied airily, waving a dismissive hand. I knew he was lying. I knew when Dad wasn't around Omer would sweet-talk Mother into giving him money. She could never tell him no but gave him whatever he wanted. And I had seen him more than once sneak into Mother's wardrobe to help himself to a plastic pill bottle of gold coins. Whenever he caught me watching him, he just winked and laughed.

Above our heads, I saw Mother come out onto our balcony and look down.

"I need something to drink!" Omer called up to her.

"Go get it yourself," Dad replied sharply.

"I'm in the middle of my game," Omer protested. "I'm about to win this hand."

A moment later, Mother lowered a tray from the balcony to the table where Omer and his friends were gambling. There were drinks for all of them on the tray. Beside me, I could feel Dad stiffen in outrage. He turned without another word and went into the building, and I knew there was going to be a fight. Dad always thought Mother was too soft on Omer. When they fought, Mother would become violent and throw things. I could feel the prickling of my skin, the hair rising on my arms. It felt the same as when there was a thunderstorm rolling in from the sea, and I could sense the electric charge in the air.

I decided to stay downstairs and sit under my willow tree for a while.

* * *

During that summer, I could feel the old silence begin to creep over me again. I could actually observe it in myself, like watching the slow formation of crystals as they climb a string dangled in salt water. Little by little, it enclosed me, hardened, obscured, until I was once again the same shadow person I'd been before school had started. I kept my head down, kept quiet, and kept myself busy and out of Mother's way.

Some days she didn't notice me at all, and though those were rather boring days, they were safe ones. She would sit at the window like a statue and hardly move other than the wringing of her hands. Other times it felt as if she had woken from a sleep and suddenly rejoined Dad and me. She would talk in long streams of words I didn't always understand, hardly pausing for breath, as if she were a great balloon and someone had unknotted her neck and let the air out. She would eat her meal with relish and smile at me between bites, with her eyes twinkling. She couldn't hold still but was constantly in motion, a flutter of scarves, a swaying of fabric. The colorful handkerchiefs at her waist reminded me of a sailboat's pennants.

On really bad days, Mother grew fierce and shrieked at us if we did anything to upset her. Nothing pleased her. She hated the food Dad cooked for her, even if it was the exact same recipe she'd greatly enjoyed just a few days before. She didn't like me staring at her. She yelled at people who weren't there, moved with agitated gestures, and pulled at the sleeves of her blouse as if her arms were unbearably itchy. She scared me on those days. I did my best to keep her happy, but it was an exhausting task because I never knew what would please her and what would set her off. Sometimes if I offered to turn on music for her, she loved it and listened with a contented smile, but on a bad day if I made the same offer, she would cry that I was pestering her and that she hated listening to music. One day I would offer her a favorite snack and she would accept it happily, and the next day she would knock the plate from my hand and scream at me to clean up the mess. A couple of minutes later she would be calm and smiling again, as if nothing had happened. The roller coaster of emotions left me constantly on edge, off balance, quivering muscles tensed for a race that would never begin.

On Saturday, Dad and I walked down to the market with our string bags. After what my friends had said about their own fathers, I found myself studying the other shoppers. I noticed, with something akin to shock, that they were all women. Men came to the market only to sell, not to buy fruit and bread and rice. When my father purchased our food, the vendors would look taken aback at first, or if they were people we often bought from, they would give my father a sort of pitying look. I had never noticed this before. In the evenings, I saw older men sitting and talking in the street while their wives prepared dinner and shouted for the children and hung clothes out to dry. My father never joined the other men in the street; he was too busy. My new awareness unsettled me and made me feel old.

I spoke to Dad about it only once, and that was without really meaning to. I came into the apartment one evening after playing outside and found him folding the freshly dried laundry, setting it in neat stacks in a basket on the floor. I leaned against the table and watched him. I was filled with a new feeling I hadn't felt before, a feeling I couldn't even put words to. I suppose, now, that it was probably shame. For a brief moment, I felt a surge of anger toward him for being so different from the other fathers. Well, no, if I were honest, I was angry with Mother for forcing Dad to take over her role. But there was no point in being angry with Mother; Dad said she couldn't help being the way she was. It was wicked to judge her. So in the end, I could only be angry at myself for feeling the way I felt.

"Aysegul says her father never cooks or cleans," I said abruptly, when at last I could no longer remain still.

"That is unfortunate," Dad replied, folding a towel into neat squares.

"She says it's—" I stopped suddenly, shifting my feet, afraid I was about to insult him.

"What is it, Ayse?" His voice was gentle.

"Women's work," I ended in a mumble.

But Dad just smiled. He set the towel on the stack and bent over to put his hand on my head. His touch was warm and reassuring, and the awful new feelings within me stilled.

"Caring for another human being is an honor," he said. "I will always take care of you."

* * *

Mother loved washing her hands under running warm water for hours at a time, and the soap made her hands whiter and whiter. She would turn the bar of soap over and over in her hands until it dissolved completely away. She could easily use an entire bar of soap with one washing. Of course, I didn't know it at the time, but now I recognize it as a compulsive disorder. To her fragile mind, having clean hands required great effort, and anything less than hours of washing would not be clean enough. If by accident she touched anything with her bare hands, she had to wash them for hours to get rid of the germs. To her thinking, germs were the cause of her many problems, and that is why she did not go out often. Inside our apartment, she was safe, but the few times she went out, all things she might touch had to be cleaned by my father. In every photograph I have of Mother, her hands are closed in tight fists to avoid touching anything.

Another funny quirk Mother had was that she couldn't go anywhere outside the apartment unless she visited the bathroom first. She would say, "You know we're going out pretty soon. Is everybody ready?"

"Yes," we would reply. "We're just waiting for you."

"Wait a minute," she would say and go into the bathroom. While she was in there, she would call out to us, "I'm coming now. Is everybody ready?"

But the funny part was that if anyone made a noise while she was getting ready to come out of the bathroom, she would have to go back in. Everything had to be quiet in order for her to come out. Omer knew she had this quirk, so if he didn't want to go to the particular place she had in mind, he would go over to the bathroom door just as she was about to come out and bang on it and shout, "Yes, we're ready now." Mother would return to the toilet. Sometimes he would make her go back and back again fifteen times, and by the time she finally came out, the event or appointment would have passed and we would have missed it, and Omer didn't have to go after all. Then Mother would complain about it for two or three hours afterward. Her complaining was a constant refrain running through my childhood, a sour note in the symphony.

One day the fire that was always smoldering beneath the surface fanned into bright flame. We had planned a rare outing to the beach that morning, but Dad got a phone call from the factory saying there was some sort of problem. He would have to go in to work unexpectedly, and the outing had to be postponed.

Mother wasn't happy. Even though she wasn't keen on going out in the first place, she was more upset by the change in plans.

"You can't be trusted! I can never rely on you!" she began shouting. "Your work is more important to you than I am!"

Dad tried to calm her down with assurances that we would go to the beach the next day. But Mother would have none of it.

"What am I supposed to do all day?" she raged. "You leave me here with children to look after and are no help to me at all!"

I thought this very unfair because it was Dad who did everything, and I never caused her a moment of work. I was very self-contained and independent, and Omer hardly qualified as a child. But Mother continued to fume and cry. Dad began to lose patience, and Omer didn't help matters by jumping into the middle of the argument. Finally, Mother shot out of her chair, snatched up a glass from the kitchen counter, and hurled it at my father.

Dad ducked, and the glass shattered against the wall. Omer laughed because she had missed her target, and this made Mother even more furious. She dove for the cupboard and began sweeping all the glasses out onto the floor. I could feel my heart lurch in my chest like a bird in a bottle. Glass flew everywhere with a terrific crash. Dad tried to grab Mother by the arms to stop her, but it made her even wilder. She screamed and swore and struggled against him, kicking broken glass across the floor in a glittering spray, and finally he had to let go of her and step back in order not to be hurt himself. He turned his head and looked directly at me with his intense blue eyes, where I cowered in the bedroom doorway.

"Go, Ayse," Dad said simply

And I did.

I didn't even stop for my shoes. I went down the stairs, across the grass, and under the willow tree, where I huddled with my knees drawn up to my chest and my arms wrapped around them. The muscles in my arms were trembling. Rocking slightly back and forth, I hummed a little to block out the sounds coming from our apartment window. I tried not to think about the neighbors coming to their windows or out onto their balconies to listen. I tried not to think about the mask of fury my mother's face had become.

The sounds ceased after a while, but I didn't venture back home. It would take time for Dad to get Mother into her bed and to sweep up the broken glass. He probably wouldn't make it in to work today after all. I rocked a little more slowly and waited for Dad to come get me. He knew where to find me. After all, this was where I always came.

Chapter Four

"Neglect not the gift that is in thee."
—*1 Timothy 4:14*

WHEN THE LONG MONTHS OF summer drew to an end, I was ready to go back to school. I had liked being with Dad again, but I no longer fit comfortably at home, and the thought saddened me. I knew I would be happier at school, though I could never admit such a thing to my father. I said good-bye to Mother. This was one of her good days, and she touched my hair and told me good-bye. I tried not to acknowledge the rush of relief I felt as Dad and I walked back to the school with my bag. Surely a good daughter wouldn't want to go, I thought guiltily. But I could feel the tight feeling leave my stomach the farther we walked from home. My neck and shoulders didn't feel so stiff, as if the crystals that had encased me all summer were shattering and dropping away. When Dad left me at the gate, his eyes were wet with unshed tears, and though I felt the wrench in my own heart, I didn't cry this time.

Looking back on it years later, I understood more deeply the turmoil my father must have felt. He was very close to me and wanted me at home with him, for I truly believed he delighted in our friendship as much as I did. I was the bright spot in his life as much as he was in mine. And yet, for my own sake, he felt he had to preserve me as best he could from my mother, to spare me from the effects of her mental illness and shield me from the fallout of her temper. What a terrible choice it must have been, to send away his little daughter, to let her go from him, and then to return home himself to the woman who had made the separation necessary. The conflicting loyalties must have torn him apart, but he never let me see it.

All the students had returned from their vacation. The bustle around the school as we all settled back in was a great contrast to the self-conscious silence of my parents' apartment. The other girls greeted me noisily and wanted to hear how my summer had gone. What had I done? What had I seen? Did I do anything exciting?

I thought of the beautiful meals my father had cooked and of how we had gone to the market together, carrying the food back, swinging it in our string bags. I thought of the interesting newspapers we had discussed and the lovely music we had listened to. I thought of his hand warm around mine as we walked. I thought of my mother lurking like a raven in her chair by the window, of shattered glass glittering on the kitchen floor.

"We went to the seaside," I lied, making my voice loud and casual. "It was very hot and boring. How was *your* summer?"

I slipped easily back into my classes. At school I didn't have to keep my head down.

* * *

I thrived on the school's routine—probably the first routine ever introduced into my life to that point. At school there were rules and structure, and far from seeing them as restricting, I saw them as protective and comforting in their predictability. There was no guesswork needed here. I knew what to expect and what was expected of me. I didn't have to stay on edge and tensed, trying to anticipate the possible outcome of any action. I was surrounded by stable adults who had important work to do and took it seriously. At school I experienced security for the first time.

I wanted to please my teachers and threw myself into my studies. I was always very bright, and I consistently earned top scores. I was keen to absorb every bit of information presented to me, and each new thing I learned opened up a host of new thoughts to me that I could then share with Dad on visiting day. I liked being able to introduce new, interesting topics in our discussions and hear what he had to say about them. It made me feel like I was contributing, keeping up my half of the conversation; and above all else, I wanted to make my father proud of me.

I had classes in English, ballet, drama, music, folk dance, and foreign languages. Languages came easily to me, the pieces slotting together in my head to form the meanings, and playing with words was like figuring out a clever puzzle. It was a game to me. And because I was petite, I did better at the dancing than some of the other girls. I also learned to overcome my shyness and enjoy the drama classes, where I could pretend to be an entirely different person. When I was acting out a story, I could let go of my own history, my own setting, and become someone new. I could shout out with my voice and receive encouragement instead of suppression. I found it exhilaratingly freeing. Sometimes it was a little difficult to give up the playacting and return to myself.

But of all the subjects we were taught, I liked music best of all. I could sing well, I loved the creative outlet it provided, and I found the flow of sound and the rise and fall of different musical instruments soothing. There was structure in music, rules to follow, and to some extent, predictability. The interactions of the different musical voices wove an interesting texture around me, like fascinating conversations that captured my imagination and lifted me out of my surroundings. Music could send me far, far away in an instant.

There were always interesting things going on in the school. It was like a gigantic entertainment center for children, and I was involved in all the programs and activities I could squeeze in. Extra activities cost extra money, but my father spared no expense so I could participate in everything that interested me.

A few months after I'd returned to school, Dad came to visiting day with momentous news.

"You have a little brother now," he said. His face was carefully blank, not smiling or frowning.

I was amazed. "I do? What is his name? What does he look like?"

"His name is Cihangir."

The name meant "conqueror of the universe" in Turkish. I thought it was rather a lot for a baby to have to live up to.

"Can I see him? Can I come to see?" I asked excitedly. This was a startling and exciting idea, since my world so far had revolved largely around me. The other children at school sometimes spoke of their younger siblings, and now I would be able to too. It was like being admitted to an exclusive club. I was a *big sister*!

"You can't come yet," Dad said slowly. "Not right away."

"Why not?"

He looked away, across the courtyard for a moment, gazing at the other children and their parents without, I thought, really seeing them.

"Things are really bad in the house right now," Dad finally said. He kept his voice low so I had to lean close to hear. He didn't have to explain to me that he was referring to Mother. He reached out a hand and smoothed my hair from my cheek. "Maybe soon, Ayse. We will hope you can come home soon."

After he left, I thought about this intently. Were things really so bad at home that they could only handle one little child at a time? To be honest, I didn't mind putting off a visit. I felt guilty for admitting it even to myself, but I wasn't thrilled at the thought of going home again. I was in no hurry to have that mantle of silence, suffocating and sour, fall over me. We hadn't discussed it, but I was thinking of asking if I could remain at school the next summer holiday. If it had been just my father at home, I would have wanted to be there. I missed him every moment we were apart. But the thought of another two months with Mother made the old churning return to my stomach. I thought about this new baby brother, living at home with Mother full time, small and vulnerable. When Dad was away at work all day, was Mother watching Cihangir? I pictured Mother picking him up with her hands swathed in her scarves. What color handkerchief would she use for the baby? Blue because he was a boy? He wouldn't be considered an object brought into the house from outside, but I pictured him crying and soiling his diapers, as I knew babies did, and tried to imagine my mother dealing with it. She would be cross and tired and overwhelmed by the sheer germiness of it all.

I decided maybe school wasn't such a bad place to be after all.

Sure enough, the next summer I was the only student at the school who didn't go home for the break. I watched all the other girls leave one by one with their parents, and then the visiting room was empty, and I was the only one left. It was a very odd feeling, as if I were a suitcase abandoned on a train platform because no one had claimed it. But I knew it was better this way. Because classes were out and most of the teachers were gone, I was allowed to spend my time pretty much however I liked. It felt disorienting to walk through the vacant rooms and not see another child. I read a lot, walked in the gardens, and played by myself in the orchard. I made daisy chains and tiaras of flowers. I ate in the kitchen with the few staff who remained over the summer, though they didn't speak to me very much, and it wasn't like eating meals with my father. But I wasn't lonely; my own imagination was entertainment enough for me. And I enjoyed having my bedroom to myself, not having to dress in front of others, and not having to share anything. This was a different sort of silence, a comfortable one, and I liked it.

The next school term, though, I did go home for a week's visit at winter break. Dad came to get me, walked home with me, and let me into the apartment just as he had before, but this time there was this new person there, and I was introduced at last to my little brother, a dark-eyed, golden-skinned little boy with a round face and very white teeth. He had a permanently puzzled look on his face, even when he smiled, as if he were trying to figure everything out about this new place.

I didn't think much of him at first. He whined a lot and couldn't really play games with me. I couldn't see that Mother really had much to do with him. Babies are nothing if not messy, and Cihangir was no exception. But Dad showed me how to feed him and keep him tidy. I made sure he didn't fall or bump his head, and I fetched his toys for him when he dropped them or threw them away. I comforted him when he cried, rocking him on my lap. Every morning that week I put his coat on him and took him on short walks in the street. I confess it was sort of like having a novel pet. I enjoyed the experience while it lasted, but when I returned to school, Cihangir was no longer a real part of my life. Like everything else to do with home, he became slightly unreal to me when I was away, far removed from my world at school.

Each time I visited home after that, Cihangir was a little bit bigger, a little more able to play with me. I grew to care for him over time, but we were not ever very close. I remember I fought with him once because he rode my bike without permission, but in general, he was a good-natured and solemn child. He had a more gentle disposition than I did. I could see in him the beginnings of the self-conscious silence I had acquired as a small child.

* * *

At some point in my childhood—I'm not sure when—I became aware of the fact that Omer Toksoz was technically my uncle, not my older brother. Little by little I became aware of some of the details I had absorbed through casual conversation. My grandmother, my mother's birth mother, had had several children by various husbands. When Omer had been about seven years old, Mother had gone to get her half brother and bring him to Istanbul. Apparently, Dad had objected because he was too old to adapt, and it wouldn't work out, and sure enough, within a year, Omer had run away, back to his parents. But Mother had gone and fetched him again, and that time he'd agreed to stay in Istanbul with her and Dad. He had always been well provided for, with Mother giving him whatever he wanted. He had expensive clothing and everything else he could desire. My parents had even bought him a car, which he wrapped around a tree the first time he drove it.

As he got older, Omer became a problem. He smoked and drank a lot and became violent when he didn't get his way. He played the guitar, and once when he was angry, he smashed it through a window, sending glass everywhere. When Mother came to her senses enough to deny him something or lecture him on his errant ways, Omer manipulated her by becoming dramatically sad and suicidal, superficially cutting his wrists, knowing that at the first sight of blood, Mother would give in to anything. Sometimes he grew violent toward her and threatened to pour gasoline over her and set fire to her like a rat. This was especially terrifying for Mother, who harbored a lifelong fear of fire. It frightened me too because I was never sure if he really meant it.

Omer was never mentally stable. He saw things, talked about things and people that weren't there, and made up stories, as if he belonged to a different world from the rest of us. He used drugs as he grew older. It seemed we went to the police station every week because of Omer. The police knew us well because Omer had frequent incidents—loud arguments, breaking glass—and the neighbors complained. They knew us well at the hospital too, where we took Omer when he tried to commit suicide for the umpteenth time. I remember Dad saying, "It would be nice if they'd *keep* him in the jail or in the hospital, so at least we'd know where he is." But Mother always went down and bailed him out. He didn't stay home for long; he came and went often. When he was home, I tended to avoid interacting much with him because of his unpredictability and violent tendencies. But I looked up to him in one sense because I recognized he was very intelligent. He always read and knew everything there was to know about politics. When he was sober, he took Cihangir and me into the city on fun outings, but it didn't happen often. I continued to think of him as my older brother.

Even with Omer away much of the time now, the slightest thing set off terrible fights at my house—an unforeseen problem, a dirty glass left in the sink, a misunderstood remark, a small disappointment, any act of stubbornness or defiance. On my visits home, I witnessed many of these altercations. Mostly it was my mother who would yell, though sometimes Dad lost his patience and shouted back. The pattern was always the same. The noise level would escalate, the tension would mount like magma rising in a volcano, and then at some point my mother would get hold of a stack of dishes or a mirror and just throw them; everything she could find, she would smash. The noise was terrific. Dad would send Cihangir and me out of the apartment to keep us from getting hurt.

I had a friend say once that we all do crazy things, but crazy people do more of them. Down in the street, listening to the sounds coming from our apartment windows, I knew that was the label people put on my mother: *crazy*. The word made my stomach hurt.

I didn't want to share my willow tree with Cihangir, so he and I slept on the street when there were fights. We would huddle in doorways, close together to keep warm, my arm serving as his pillow. The stone of the buildings still held the heat from the sun, and it radiated back into the air at night to help keep us warm. Cihangir would tuck his little head into the crook of my elbow and sleep like a puppy, quite at home on the hard cement. I wondered sometimes what Cihangir did when I was away at school. Did Dad send him out on the street then too, all alone? I never asked him. We never talked about it or asked each other why Dad tolerated Mother's abuse. That was what it was, I recognize now, but at the time, of course, we didn't put a label on it. It was just Mother being Mother. The rest of us just had to make allowance for her.

The next morning Cihangir and I would awaken stiff from sleeping on the doorstep. The neighbors would find us and give us hot, sweet tea and biscuits, and then they would bring us back to our apartment and talk to my parents. They would say, "This isn't the way to raise children." But there were no social services back then, and people didn't tend to interfere much with others' domestic lives. The neighbors would go away again—until the next time. We didn't think much about it,

Cihangir and I. We were used to it, but by the time I was eleven or twelve years old, it became embarrassing.

At the end of every fight, Mother and Dad would make up. I liked the making-up part of the cycle because we would go out to dinner, and Mother would splurge. We bought new dishes to replace the ones she had smashed—never referring to the reason for the purchase, of course. We went on short trips with rented bicycles and went on shopping sprees and just played together. I loved going to an expensive restaurant near the seaside in Istanbul. I had always found the blue sea so comforting. I felt as if all that ocean water could wash away the pain in my heart. Certainly washing the pain with my tears was not enough.

Mother bought Cihangir and me clothing and toys. I guess she was trying to make up for everything—the shattered glass, the sleeping on the street, the excruciating kindness of the neighbors. I accepted the gifts and the outings for what they were: peace offerings for a peace that never lasted more than a week or two. But I learned to take what I could get while it was offered.

I remember one time when she was trying to make up with Dad, she attempted to cook, even though she was afraid of the stove. She put a chicken and some vegetables in the pressure cooker. I don't know what went wrong, but suddenly the thing exploded with a *kaboom*. I screamed, thinking a bomb had gone off. There was chicken on the ceiling, vegetables everywhere. The neighbors came running, thinking the butane gas had exploded in our apartment. It scared me so badly that years later, when my husband gave me a beautiful new pressure cooker, I couldn't bring myself to touch it. To me, it looked as frightening as a nuclear warhead. It remains today in my basement in a box, forever unused.

***

I didn't come home from school very often. My father continued to visit me weekly on visiting day, and he often brought news of things my teachers never spoke about. He always read the newspapers and listened to the radio and then shared with me what he had learned. I don't know if he did this out of interest in my education or because he just felt the need to talk about these disturbing things with someone and he had no one else to turn to. It was a time of violence and unrest in Turkey.

He told me of bombings of government buildings and assassinations that had occurred. The political climate of the country was rapidly changing. There was martial law in Istanbul, with the military taking over the role of the policing authority and the court because the civil authorities couldn't function properly. My teachers were not always happy with the things Dad told me; they thought I was too young to know about such events. But I drank in every bit of news. I developed a keen interest in politics and current events at a young age.

One visiting day, my father's face was grim, and so were the faces of the other visiting parents. Their smiles didn't seem as confident or reassuring as usual, and the room where we visited was filled with low, tense voices. Speaking to me as he would an adult, as was his habit, Dad explained that there was more trouble in the country. Four American servicemen had been kidnapped. It was the first time I'd heard the word *anarchy*, and he had to explain it to me. He told me how, just before I was born, the tensions in Turkey between the government and the opposition had nearly exploded into civil war. Students had led riots in the streets. Prime Minister Adnan Menderes was removed from power and hanged, and the parliament had been dissolved. Free elections had been instated, but now political violence was increasing again, and the economy was deteriorating. I didn't understand all he told me. All I knew was the storm was rising outside my school; the skin on my arms prickled again with worry and—I admit—excitement. There were big things happening outside the walls of my school, and I wished I could be out there in the middle of them.

That afternoon, the principal lectured us students on the failure of the economy. Most of it went over our heads. The only thing we came away with was the knowledge that we were very lucky our parents could afford to send us to this school, which was apparently very expensive. Other children in Istanbul were not as lucky as we were.

Not long after that, Dad told me the elected conservative Demirel government of Turkey had been forced to resign.

"We have a coalition government in power now. They are supported by the armed forces," he explained.

"What will that mean for us?" I asked. I felt the lack of a radio acutely. Our teachers never discussed such matters in detail, and I felt so cut off from all that was happening.

"Nothing will change for you here," Dad said. "But remember, Ayse, there will always be those who are in need of your help and protection. You must always be a good citizen and care for your fellow beings."

I took those words to heart and wanted to be a good citizen, but it was difficult to know exactly how to do that when I was trapped inside the school walls. I tried to put it into practice by being kind to the other students around me, even those who were not kind to me. I viewed my father as the ideal and tried to conduct myself patiently and wisely as I thought he would do. More often than not, though, I disappointed myself by letting my temper or impatience get the upper hand.

Compared to the instability and turbulence in Turkey, my sheltered life was rather stolid. Prime Minister Nihat Erim gave way to Ferit Melen a year later, and just a year after that, Melen gave way to Naim Talu. In 1973, the country held a general election, and Dad's smile was broad as he informed me the next visiting day that civilian rule was now in place. But there would be six changes of prime minister in the next seven years.

* * *

One spring morning in 1974, one of the teachers came into our bedroom as we were dressing for the day.

"Ayse, you are to go to the principal's office."

I paused, my stockings in my hand, and stared at her. I couldn't imagine why I was being summoned.

"You're in trouble." One of my friends laughed. But I was never in trouble, so I knew there must be news of some kind. I finished dressing and hurried to the office with my heart doing flip-flops in my chest. Had something happened to my family? I remembered how Omer had threatened to set my mother on fire and wondered if he had finally done it. Or perhaps he really had succeeded in killing himself this time. Maybe Cihangir had been struck by a car. The traffic was always heavy on our street. I didn't let myself think of something bad happening to Dad—it just couldn't, that was all.

But it wasn't my family. The principal, in the same deep and kindly voice with which he had welcomed me to the school nearly five years before, told me I was leaving it. Just like that, as suddenly as the day I'd come.

"What do you mean? Why?" I asked, astounded.

"You are to pack your things and be ready. Your father is coming to get you this morning."

"Have I done something wrong?"

"If you hurry, you will have time to tell your friends good-bye."

There was to be no explanation.

Dad arrived, looking a little sheepish. I was waiting in the visiting room with my luggage. My things no longer fit into my one original bag, though I still had it. I had said a hasty good-bye to the other girls and didn't know if I would ever see any of them again.

"What's happening?" I asked Dad. "Is everything all right?"

"Yes, yes. It's just that we are moving to a different part of Istanbul," Dad said, picking up my bags. "We have a new apartment on the fifth floor of a building in the district of Besiktas."

I had no say in the matter, not any more than I'd had as the little girl who had come to this school so long ago.

Chapter Five

> *"We wait for light, but behold obscurity; for
> brightness, but we walk in darkness."*
> —Isaiah 59:9

BESIKTAS WAS SITUATED ON THE shores of the blue Bosphorus, with its
Italian-looking architecture and lovely parks. It was once the home of
the famous sailor Barbarossa and was where the Byzantines had built
their holiday homes. *Besiktas*, which means "cradle stone," is said to
have been the site of a Byzantine church, now long gone, that housed
a relic, a stone taken from the stable in Bethlehem where Jesus was
born. I was familiar with Jesus; Muslims saw him as a great prophet,
and Dad had told me the story of His humble birth. I couldn't imagine
anyone being born in a primitive stable. Even though I'd slept in some
uncomfortable places myself, at least I'd always had a warm home to go
back to afterward. I hoped His parents had sold the gold, frankincense,
and myrrh and bought a decent house with it.

In spite of the beautiful area of the city in which it was located, my
new public school was very different from the privileged private school
I had grown used to over the last five years. It was a square block of a
building with no grace or beauty about it. There was nothing special
about the school, and there was no special treatment, no drama or
ballet, and no extra activities. There was no lovely garden of flowers
or orchard of apricots to sit in. The children there were ordinary, not
wealthy or privileged in any way. We had our studies and nothing else.
It was difficult to get used to, and I didn't attempt to make friends with
any of the other children. It seemed I always had a heavy rock sitting in
my stomach; I didn't know to call it depression.

When I had left my boarding school in 1974, I had been leery of returning to live with Mother full time, but she seemed different now. She didn't mutter to herself as much, and she responded calmly when I spoke to her. She still didn't help with the cooking or cleaning, and she still had her chair by the window overlooking our new street, but she seemed happier and didn't yell or throw things as much. At times, she even caressed my shoulder as she walked past and smiled and spoke in a quiet, loving tone. I wasn't sure what to make of it.

When I mentioned to Dad that Mother must be feeling better, he replied, "She isn't on medication, but she is getting help through counseling."

Whatever it was, it was helping. Mother became more like those mothers I'd seen visiting my friends at the school. At dinner she asked me how my day went and listened to my answers. She questioned Omer about where he went with his friends in the evening (he didn't reply, but at least she asked). She helped Cihangir cut his meat, and once, when my father said something funny, she actually laughed. We all stared at her because it was a sound we almost never heard. I don't think Cihangir knew she was capable of it, judging from the look of wonder on his round face.

Mother even praised me when I brought home good grades. However, her praise was not important to me. I only valued my father's opinion of me. I recognized how much he did for Cihangir and me, far beyond the traditional role of an ordinary father. My initial shame had long since dissolved in my admiration for him, for his willingness to do whatever it took to care for his family. At that age, the only reward or show of appreciation I could give my father was excellent grades through hard work and study. But I must admit that seeing my mother happier brought happiness to my heart. She went with us on bicycle rides and on walks along the seaside. She spoke kindly, and it was as if the invisible people she had always argued with had been left behind at our old apartment. It was very nice for a time, but I never fully trusted it. I never let my guard down. I was always acutely aware of where she was and what she was doing, like a shadow in the corner of my eye, and I tried my best to keep her in good spirits.

On her good days, we often went shopping. Mother loved to buy me pretty dresses. On good days, I could get her to do anything for me. Once, I even made her buy me a tiara. I loved the shiny stones on that tiara; it looked so beautiful displayed on the white veil of a wedding gown, and I had to have it. All I had to do was ask Mother to buy it for me, and she couldn't say no.

She would comb my hair and put pretty pins in it with great care. Oh, how I enjoyed her light touch. She had beautiful hands, very soft and white, the hands of a delicate woman. It was hard for me to reconcile those soft hands with the same hands that had sometimes slapped and beaten me as a young child. On such days, when she was gentle in her touch, there were just the two of us in the entire world. But the happy moments never lasted long.

Of course, I loved being back with my father again too. He was the only constant thing in my ever-changing life. When he returned from his long workday, he and I would spend every moment together. Dad treated me as if I were a miniature adult, and I liked the feelings of pride and confidence that gave me. He listened to what I had to say as if it were important, and he told me things as though he trusted me; I like to think it was because he valued my opinion. I knew the teachers at my old school had thought I was bright. The woman who had quizzed me about what Dad and I talked about on visiting days had more than once struck up conversations with me about current events and politics and had seemed surprised by my informed answers. I enjoyed such conversations; I much preferred serious debate over the noisy chatter and games of other children.

It was different, though, sharing Dad with Cihangir. I was used to receiving his undivided attention. Life at home had a rather awkward and unreal element to it. After five years without parents, I suddenly had them again, and it took getting used to.

While we were in Besiktas, Greek Cypriots staged a coup d'état, and within a week, the Turks took control of Northern Cyprus. I remember hearing about it on the radio and discussing it with my father, trying to understand the causes and effects. It was all we talked about for a while. The United States imposed a sales embargo on Turkey in retaliation, which was to last for four years. This embargo impacted many of our neighbors but left my family relatively untouched in comparison. Wealth can cushion people from the stark realities that others around them can't escape, but I was too young to fully grasp how privileged my position was. And I had other battles with which to occupy myself.

We lived in Besiktas only a short time. Summer holidays came, and school was over. And so was the fragile truce in my house. Mother's invisible opponents returned, and she raged at them more and more frequently. I would watch her eyes because when she became psychotic, her eyes would move strangely, as if she were looking back and forth between objects none of us could see. When the eye movements began, that was my signal to take cover. Mother grew hysterical at those times, shouting at nothing and throwing her arms into the air as if fighting off real attackers. She often looked nervous and worn out. Daily life was too much for her. Everything and everyone was against her, and she was afraid of life. I tried my best to comfort her, but sometimes all I could do was lie low and let her go.

No matter where I was or what I was doing, I always kept my ears pricked. It was as if I could always sense at every moment where Mother was and what mood she was in, as if my skin picked up radar signals. Even though I was very careful to do nothing wrong and kept Cihangir quietly out of the way, Mother still found fault with everything. She would shout at us and shove us—or worse, ignore us completely. I kept thinking that if only we did a little better, if we only talked softer or more promptly did what she told us to do, it would be fine; she wouldn't act out. But it didn't work. Mother spent more and more time in her chair overlooking the road. One day she struck me hard across the face, something she hadn't done for several months. It was as if that action started a mudslide, the first trickle picking up momentum and turning into a crashing torrent. Both verbal and physical abuse became a natural part of daily life.

How could one person cause so much harm? Mother was toxic. All the yelling, all the noise was too much. It was against my nature, but I also began to yell. I wasn't a silent little girl anymore. I was on the verge of becoming a teenager, and I found I was able to fight back. Recognizing that power in myself was exhilarating. My temper grew into a thing to behold. And when the battle became too intense, I was able simply to escape. I would just go out and not return for several hours. When I finally came home, I would find Mother sitting there crying.

"I don't feel well," she once told me through her tears. "I don't know what is happening to me. I know what I'm doing isn't right. I know I'm not supposed to do these things, but something comes over me, and it just comes out. I don't know what to do about it."

Sometimes my heart would break for her, but other times I felt a cold shell around my heart, refusing to let me feel any sympathy for her. As I got older, the shell would appear more and more often because I became exhausted with the routine. But I knew the part I was to play.

"It's all right," I would dutifully assure her.

"It isn't my fault."

"I know."

"I promise I won't do it again," she would say.

"Of course, Mother. It's all right."

Then, for a time, we'd eat and play and spend money and all would be well, and then one or two weeks later, *wham*; it would happen again. I spent my life trying to keep one step ahead of her moods. Looking back on it now, as an adult, I can see how futile that was. Nothing I did could have made a difference one way or another. I didn't have a word for her condition then, but I suppose now we would recognize it as schizophrenia (and I think Omer probably had it as well). Mother never acknowledged she was ill. She refused to take medication. In her mind, everyone else was always at fault, and to some extent, I believed her.

Guilt is a thin soup to raise a child on. So is fear.

One day Mother was ranting in one of her fits, screaming that someone was trying to kill her. I remember Cihangir was hiding in the bedroom, and Dad and I were calmly trying to carry on with the task of making dinner, as if nothing were happening. Suddenly, there was a loud bang on our apartment door.

When my father opened it, a man rushed in. It was the doorman from downstairs. The look on his face was wild, and he clutched a long stick in his hands.

"What is it? Where is he?" he cried, looking this way and that.

Dad hurried over to him with his palms held outward. "Where is who? What's the matter?"

"I heard—someone is attacking her!"

The doorman caught sight of Mother, huddled and screaming on her chair with no one near her. He stopped in confusion and lowered the stick.

Dad put a hand on the man's shoulder and turned him right around again.

"Turkan is just hallucinating," he explained patiently, his ears turning a bit red. "No one is hurting her. No one is trying to kill her. But thank you very much for coming to her rescue."

The doorman went away again, and Dad told Mother in a terse voice, "If you keep doing that, no one will listen to you anymore."

But it happened again and again, in the way of the classic story *The Boy Who Cried Wolf.* The doorman continued to run to her rescue every time. Dad would reassure him and send him away. And Mother would continue to scream.

Like me, Dad learned to live in silence.

* * *

Omer continued to be a vague presence in our lives, sometimes there, more often not. Dad wanted to make something of him and opened up a clothing store for Omer to run in Istanbul. It was a very generous offer and could have set him up for life. But Omer had other ideas. Within a month, he sank the store financially. He gave away the stock and often brought home clothing for me, still in its plastic wrappers and smelling new and lovely. He once placed many beautiful necklaces around my neck, and I danced around in them, thinking how lovely I looked. At some point, though, Omer disappeared altogether, leaving the store a ruin, and Dad told me he had moved away to the south of Turkey. I was both glad and sorry he'd gone.

When we left Besiktas in the late summer of 1974, we moved back to the same old apartment building in Levent we'd lived in when I was small. I had finished grade school and was about to enter secondary school (which would be the equivalent of seventh grade). At about this time, Mother began to act even stranger than usual. She became paranoid. One day she looked at me and said, "Who is this young woman in our home?"

Dad straightened and looked at her with a funny expression. "That's our daughter," he said.

"I have no daughter."

"Don't you recognize her, Turkan?"

"Oh yeah, I recognize her," Mother said. "She's our daughter." She turned away and continued with what she had been doing.

Dad and I just looked at each other while chills ran up my spine and across my scalp.

But a few days later, she did it again. She didn't recognize me. This happened with increasing regularity until she was saying it two or three times a day. It always gave me an eerie feeling. Even though I knew it was her illness speaking, it still made me feel like a ghost in my own home.

Then she started accusing Dad of having an affair with a young woman right in front of her, and she meant me. She thought I was a stranger intruding in her home. She no longer knew me at all. I would look into her blank eyes, hear the accusation in her voice, and it would shake me so much that it seemed I no longer even knew myself. If my own mother didn't know me, I had no anchor around which to center myself.

Finally it got to a point where my father couldn't handle it anymore. They had been married for about eighteen years, and he had patiently put up with Mother's craziness for all that time. But finally, it all snapped.

Late one evening, they started arguing in the bedroom. I could hear them. In the past, I had just shrugged my shoulders and ignored it. I thought everybody's parents slept separately and everybody argued in their homes. I had never seen anything else and thought it was normal. But this time the fight sounded different.

"I'm not going to tolerate this anymore," Dad shouted. "I'm leaving you."

I sat up straighter at my desk, where I had been doing homework. He had never said *that* before.

Mother started crying.

"Don't leave me," she wept. "How will I survive without you?"

I thought this a romantic thing to say, until she followed it with, "I have no money of my own."

"I can't do this anymore," Dad repeated. I had never heard his voice with that kind of tremor in it before. I left my room and crept closer to their bedroom door to listen to this unusual fight. I felt sick to my stomach and tucked my fists into my armpits, hugging myself.

"We've been married so many years. It's such a waste to throw it all away," she protested, her voice rising in that way that made the hair on my arms stand up.

"I'm sorry; my mind is made up."

"If you leave, you take the creatures in this house with you," Mother cried. "I don't ever want to see any of you again." There was a great crash, as if the window had smashed. She must have thrown something through it.

"These are not cats!" Dad hissed. "These are people. Don't they mean anything to you?"

"I don't want them in my house," Mother shouted back.

"In the eyes of God, I made a promise to watch over them, and I'm going to keep my promise until I give my last breath," Dad said.

The door flew open, and he came out of the room. I jumped back guiltily, caught eavesdropping, but he didn't seem to notice. His face was drawn tight with anger and sorrow, and his eyes flashed blue.

"Put on your shoes. We're leaving," he told me shortly.

"Where are we going?" I asked.

"You have to go back to your parents," he said.

I could only stand there and stare at him dumbly. "My what? My parents?" I repeated stupidly.

His face softened with a profound sadness, and he looked suddenly old and tired. He took me by the elbow. "Come into the living room."

We went into the other room. I could hear Mother wailing loudly from the bedroom. Dad drew his hands tiredly down his face then turned to me with the bleakest look I'd ever seen. He seemed to have grown shorter, folding in on himself. From the corner of my eye, I saw Cihangir creep into the room, watching us with wide, frightened eyes. He too could tell this fight wasn't ordinary.

"There is no way to tell you this gently; I'll just say it. Ayse, you and your brother are adopted," Dad said flatly.

I couldn't say anything, only stared at him.

"We adopted you many years ago because we couldn't have children of our own. But your mother didn't want to adopt you legally; it was not made official. You are related to her by blood but not to me. I cannot keep you anywhere by myself because that would be illegal. You are both minors, and you have to go back to your parents in Karaman."

It felt for a moment as if a great pillow had smothered my brain, and I could barely hear or see. I reached out to catch hold of the back of a chair and clung to it. All I could think was, *Where is Karaman?* I had never heard of it. Then the pillow lifted, and sound surged into my ears once more. My mother wailed down the hall like a siren. I felt tears start down my cheeks and saw them mirrored in Dad's eyes. I looked down at Cihangir and saw he was sobbing. Panic overtook me, and I began spitting out questions like bullets, not even waiting for Dad to answer them.

"What are you talking about? What happened? How did it happen? What do you mean, I'm related to her but not to you? Why can't you keep us?" And then the frantic feeling was replaced by a wave of fury. "You're a liar! You're both liars. It isn't true."

"I'm sorry, but it is true."

"I don't trust you. I don't trust any of you."

Dad's shoulders fell, and he shook his head. "Be that as it may, we have to leave tonight."

Mother rushed down the hallway and into the living room, her face livid, her hair standing out in black waves, the embodiment of my nightmares. I actually jumped behind Dad to shield myself from her. "Good!" Mother screamed, and her voice was like shards of glass against my skin. "Good riddance! Get out of here, all of you!"

I was wearing a dress that night. It was my favorite one that I was rather proud of, navy blue with puffed sleeves. My brother had on short pants and a T-shirt. I watched Dad pick up his jacket. He took money out of his wallet, thrust it into Mother's hands, and said tightly, "This will be the last time we will have any dealings with one another. We're leaving. This is it."

And just like that, the three of us walked down the stairs to the street. We saw the lights in the building turn on one by one when the ruckus woke the neighbors. We didn't worry about them because we knew they already knew the screaming was a daily event in our household.

Above us, my mother opened the window and threw the trash can after us. It was a metal can, and it went crashing down onto the street, making me flinch. I remember the sound distinctly. I hated noise; there had always been such terrific noise in my childhood, and I had grown to hate disturbing sounds. The can rolled on the street behind us, and the lid rolled off in another direction. Mother yelled at the top of her lungs, "Take your mistress with you! Don't come back! I hate you!"

Dad reached down and took Cihangir's hand. We kept walking without looking back.

"I gave the best years of my life to you!" Mother went on screaming, her voice growing fainter behind us. "My beautiful soft hair became like a stiff broom!"

Dad took my hand with his other one. His skin was cold around mine. We turned the corner and left the street. Cihangir was only about six or seven years old, and he didn't have a clue what was happening, but I knew, and I walked with stomping, determined feet to hide the trembling in my legs. We went to the station and purchased bus tickets and waited for the bus. It was late at night by this time and beginning to grow chilly. We could only get a back-row seat on the bus. It was the most uncomfortable fifteen-hour ride I've ever taken in my life.

As we rode through the night, lurching with clashing gears, Dad sat with his arm around my brother—he didn't try to touch me again—and he spoke in low tones.

"Your mother—you have to understand. She was adopted too as a baby." He told us the story of the young, unmarried mother, Havva, and the judge who had taken in her unwanted infant. I couldn't see why this had anything to do with me, but I couldn't help listening.

"When she was seventeen, Turkan found her birth mother. Her mother had married—she married nine times in all, in fact—and had had other children, who were now grown and living in Cukurbag. It's a small village of about two or three hundred people in the south of Turkey, not far from the Mediterranean. Later, Turkan and I married, but we couldn't have children. She wanted a child so badly. Your mother went to Cukurbag and brought her half brother Omer home to raise, but it was never successful. He was too old when we first got him, and he was never happy with us. When he became a handful as a teenager, Turkan decided she wanted to try a daughter, a younger girl she could raise. She went to her half brother Mustafa in Cukurbag and told him she wanted his daughter. You were two and a half at the time. It happens, sometimes, that people give their children to relatives to raise. It isn't that unusual."

I supposed I had heard of such things before, but not in connection with anyone I knew and certainly not in connection with *me*. I didn't respond. I could feel hysteria building in my chest, but I swallowed it down and stared at my own hollow-eyed reflection in the window.

"When an older person asks you for something, you give it to them," Dad said simply. "He and his wife gave you to her. Don't judge them harshly. They were very poor, Ayse, and they thought we could give you a better life. Turkan brought you back to Istanbul, and we raised you as our own. We never formally adopted you, but you know I love you as a daughter."

Did I? Did I know such a thing? I was too stunned to reply, too hurt, too bewildered. I tried to tell myself, *Of course he loves you. This is Dad!* But apparently nothing was what I thought it was. Could I truly trust that his love for me wasn't a sham as well? As I sat fighting my internal battle, my father continued to explain.

"As your mother's condition grew worse—well, you know what it was like. I had to save you from her. So even though it wasn't usual for a girl to be sent away for an education, I put you in the boarding school. But with you gone, your mother was bored," Dad murmured, almost as if talking to himself. "She wanted me to bring you back. But I said, 'I'm not bringing that child back home.' Your mother said, 'I'll show you!' and she jumped on the bus and went back to Cukurbag. She went to see Mustafa again and said, 'I need a little boy this time, not more than two years old.' Your . . . your biological parents had four other children. They gave her one of their sons, and she brought him back to Istanbul and named him Cihangir." Dad leaned closer to me and said, "Cihangir didn't go to boarding school. He had to put up with a lot more at home than you did."

I felt he was lecturing me for being ungrateful. I didn't care. I continued resolutely to pretend to ignore him. I didn't even know the meaning of the word *biological*. But I understood he was telling me that Cihangir was my real little brother, not pretend like he and Mother were pretend. His words painted a picture for me, a strange and terrible picture I had never known existed. I had been born in a poor village. My real parents, Turkan's half brother and his wife, were uneducated laborers who now lived not far from Cukurbag in a place called Karaman, a city of several thousand people at the northern foot of the Taurus mountains. Omer was living in Karaman now too. My parents were named Mustafa and Fatma Kizil. I had an older brother, Mehmet, another younger brother named Mustafa, and a younger sister, Hatice. It appeared I had belonged to the club of Big Sisters most of my life and never known it.

"You are related by blood to Turkan but not to me. The adoptions were never made formal," my father repeated. "I have no legal claim to you. That is why you must go back to your parents. If I tried to keep you myself, the authorities would take you away from me."

"How would the authorities know?" Cihangir asked from the other side of Dad.

"Turkan would send them. She would say that as your aunt she has a stronger claim to you."

"But she wouldn't. She doesn't want us," Cihangir said flatly.

My father's hair turned completely white on that bus trip from Istanbul.

Section Two
Raising My Voice

Chapter Six

"It is better to dwell in the wilderness, than with
a contentious and an angry woman."
—*Proverbs 21:19*

THOUGH DAYTIME IN THE SUMMER was scorching hot, it was cold at night, and we were very uncomfortable on the bus. We had no clothing but Dad's jacket and whatever we had been wearing when we'd walked out of the apartment. Dad took a newspaper and put layers of newspaper sheets on us to make a blanket. I shivered with shock as much as with cold. What was ahead of us? Why was it taking so long to get there? I had so many questions, but I stayed silent. I was stunned, sad, hurt, and confused. I felt as if I were in a bad dream, and I wanted to wake up so it would all go away. I wanted to go home. *Mother's abuse was probably better than what I'm going through right now*, I thought. I wanted to go back to my bed. I couldn't believe my beloved father, my favorite person in the world, wasn't my real father. He had deceived me all these years. That Mother had, yes, I believed; I never trusted her anyway. But *Dad?* All this time, he had known this terrible secret and never told me.

This hurt started to change during the long ride to fury that I directed at myself as well as at them. How could I not have known? Why hadn't I realized the truth when I'd returned home that one visit to meet my new baby brother and found not an infant but a toddler? Was I really so clueless? So gullible to have believed the fantasy? Why did I *care* so much? It wouldn't hurt so much if I could stop caring.

I tried to picture Mother, her chin held high, her handkerchiefs fluttering at her waist, riding across Turkey alone on a bus to come for me and hauling me all the way back. This was the woman who could not cook or clean for herself. This was the woman who could not shop at the market for her own food. Where had she gotten the energy and determination to do it? Why did I not remember it?

Then again, what was more believable—that she had come for me on the bus or that she had gone through the ultimately germy process of conceiving and giving birth to a child?

In time, after changing buses several times, exhausted and spent, we came to Karaman. The houses were of stone or earth, and the roads were narrow and winding. It looked as foreign to me as the surface of the moon.

"Karaman is a very old place," Dad said, leaning past me to peer out the dusty window. "It was here before the third century BC, but it wasn't named Karaman until the thirteenth century."

All I could do was look at him and think, *A history lesson now? Really?*

The bus finally stopped at the side of the rough road. My father led us off the bus, and we stood looking down the hill at a collection of miserable-looking houses. They were made of the same dry, pale stone as the desert surrounding Karaman. But the stone wasn't like the stone of Istanbul; it no longer looked like lemon or cream or butter to me. It just looked like dirt. I saw a goat casually walking along the lane ahead of us, its hip bones jutting sharply under its grimy hide. Dad prodded me in the back, and we walked down through the barren, abandoned-looking streets. The smells were unfamiliar. The sand and heat were so different from Istanbul's tree-lined boulevards. I had never seen such poverty, such *dust,* except in pictures in my geography textbook. I could not belong in such a place. The idea was too fantastic.

We came to a little dwelling made of mud and straw, a growth rising out of the earth, with hardly a distinction where wall ended and ground began. It listed to one side, and the little glass windows were covered with cheap fabric. They didn't resemble anything like the expensive curtains we had in my home. The door was a plank of wood held in place with old metal. Dad stopped. We stood looking at the house. It was very small and dilapidated compared to our nice home in Istanbul. The idea that Cihangir and I had relatives in this place was outrageous.

As we stood there, a short, rugged, suntanned lady and a taller, slim man came out of the house and just stood looking back at us. I saw nothing familiar in their simple, rural faces. Their clothing was clean but rough. The man, who had a bushy black mustache and narrow eyes, wore a dusty pale shirt that hung untucked over his knee-worn pants. The woman wore a shapeless dress with trousers beneath it, and she had tied a dark scarf tightly around her face, hiding her hair. I noticed a little girl, just a small little child, clinging to the woman's skirt, watching us from behind her with wide, brown eyes. My brain was too numb to remember the names Dad had told me. I told myself, *This is my father. That is my mother.* I looked at the tiny girl and thought, *That is my sister. They kept her and gave me away.*

Dad went up to the couple and said simply, "Things are not going well anymore. I left Turkan."

They did not ask who he was or who Cihangir and I were. They didn't ask who Turkan was or what we were doing here. My heart fell as I realized his story must be true. My father knew them and had known where they lived. He had led us straight to their hut unerringly. They knew us. My brain struggled with the idea that my elegant, well-educated father had ever interacted with such people, that he had any connection with them or this place.

Dad gestured for Cihangir and me to come closer. I could hardly get my feet to move. The man and woman stepped aside to let us into the house. They still hadn't said anything, and I wondered if they could speak. It was dim inside the little house, and it smelled funny. The floor was dirt. The walls were dirt painted white. There were only two rooms and a little shack in the back for a kitchen. There was absolutely no furniture in the main room, none at all. Around the edges of the room on the floor were placed faded fabric cushions, which I later learned were stuffed with hay. The ceiling was low, and Dad and the man had to stoop slightly.

Dad coughed and cleared his throat.

"I have brought the children back. But I would like to remain with your household. I would like to build a small room behind your house that I can stay in."

This startled me and made my heart jump in my chest. I thought he had come to drop us off and leave us behind like unwanted parcels. But he was staying! He had left his career, his home, his wife, his entire life, and he was going to stay with us. Even though I was swamped with anger, I still felt relief.

The man and woman looked at each other and then at Dad.

"You are a chemical engineer," the man said, and his accent was strange to my ears. "You have a good education and a good income. You have lived all your life in Istanbul."

"Yes," Dad said, unperturbed.

"You won't be happy here. You won't be able to work as an engineer here. You'll be bored."

"I made a covenant with God that I would watch over these children, and I will do it," Dad said. "May I stay?"

They gave their reluctant permission. I am sure they thought he only meant to stay for a little while. He stayed for eight years.

Half a life later, I found a scripture in Numbers 30:2: "If a man vow a vow unto the Lord, or swear an oath to bind his soul with a bond; he shall not break his word, he shall do according to all that proceedeth out of his mouth." My father lived up to this exhortation all of his life, though I doubt he'd ever read it.

* * *

In that little house in Karaman, Dad and the man sat down on two of the cushions, and Cihangir sat next to Dad, leaning against him, as if trying to reassure himself that Dad really was there and was staying. Dad made polite inquiries about people, speaking names I had never heard him mention before, and the man, Mustafa, answered in short replies. His wife moved silently about the little room they used as a kitchen, preparing food, I assumed, but I didn't go to investigate or help. I stood to one side, hardly listening to Dad's conversation. The little girl, my sister, stood staring at me as if I were something exotic in a store window, and I found it difficult to keep from looking at her.

That first night was a revelation. As the sun set, the tiny house filled with people. Their voices were harsh to me, their accents unfamiliar, their clothing poor. Two boys—my two other brothers—came in, one of them perhaps a year older than I, the other two years younger. Even I couldn't deny their resemblance to Cihangir. They had the same roundish faces, the same handsome dark eyes. I found myself searching their faces and comparing them to Mustafa and then to Dad. I had to admit Cihangir looked more like them and Mustafa than he did Dad. It felt like a traitorous thought.

The boys had marbles in their hands, which caught Cihangir's eye, and soon he was enticed away into a game. I kept to one corner, watching these people with an anthropologist's detachment and saying nothing. I felt as if I were watching a documentary of a laborer's life in southern Turkey, nothing to do with me.

When the prayer call was sounded, the prayer rugs came out. I had seen such things, of course, but we had never observed them in our home. Dad stood to one side with eyes downcast respectfully as the others went through the ritual. Cihangir and I followed Dad's example. A few people cast curious looks at us, but no one said anything about nonparticipation.

When they were finished, the woman—my mother—put a synthetic cloth down on the floor and brought out a huge round metal tray. On the tray, there was a copper pot, and in it there were beans and a little bit of stewed meat with bones. Several wooden spoons stood in the pot. The spices didn't smell familiar. Everybody dashed to sit on the floor and put the cloth over their knees. They each took a wooden spoon from the pot and dug right in. I waited in the corner for my dinner to arrive. No one noticed me. They all ate out of the common pot, heedless of germs. Even Dad sat and partook with them as casually as if he were seated at our elegant dining table at home. Half an hour passed by, people finished eating, and the woman took the tray and cloth and left. I sat there, still thinking she was bringing me something. When she came back from the kitchen empty-handed, I was shocked.

I called her name. "Mrs. Fatma, when do I eat?"

"Oh," she said, looking surprised. "We just did."

My dad heard me and came over to my corner.

"This is how they eat," he explained gently. "Tomorrow you'd better come quickly with spoon in hand and join in."

I couldn't help myself. I was exhausted and hungry and lost. The word *tomorrow* made my heart sink, implying as it did that this terrible nightmare wasn't going to end. I began to cry like a small child.

"I hate all of you," I cried. "I don't trust any of you. I don't know why I'm here. I don't belong here. I'll run away."

"Now, Ayse—" Dad began.

"No. I'll never fit in. You just watch. I'll go away from here. You can't keep me here." I started to run from the room and then stopped, feeling stupid. I had nowhere to run to.

Chapter Seven

"I will never leave thee, nor forsake thee."
—*Hebrews 13:5*

MY LIFE HAD BEEN FULL of changes, so I didn't know why this particular one shook me so much. I found my new life in my new home very troubling and uncomfortable. I hated my biological parents. I hated their lifestyle. I hated that they weren't learned and didn't know how to eat with proper utensils. To my Istanbul-trained ears, they didn't even know how to speak properly. I disliked everything about them, and I didn't want to acknowledge they had any part in my life, or I in theirs. For a long time, I thought of them by their first names, Fatma and Mustafa, and not as Mother and Father. They were not modern, and the females covered their heads, which I had never been raised to do. Even at such a young age, I was scornful of them and their backward ways. Mustafa could not even read and write. Once he had been forced, as an adult, to attend an evening school to learn to read, but he had rebelled and burned down the school, and that was the end of his education.

For their part, my parents must have thought I was a species from another planet. I disdained their food, their communal sleeping arrangements, the very house they lived in. I showed no respect, did not address them deferentially, and did not cover my head. I didn't know how to do simple things around the house or understand the nuances of the customs. Even though back in Istanbul I had been a fairly adept cook, I couldn't manage to transfer those skills to this foreign and rustic setting. I would catch Fatma casting sideways glances at me, a puzzled look mingled with frustration on her round face.

The more I detested Fatma and Mustafa, the more I clung to Dad. I often wouldn't eat with the family. I would go instead to his room. Dad had built a tiny room out of mud behind the house, building up the walls in layers like adobe. As I'd watched him build it, I'd wondered how this city-born man had learned to do such a thing and thought he must just be very clever to figure it out on his own. I greatly admired his ingenuity.

In his little room, he had a narrow bed, a table, and two chairs, like—I thought with pride—a civilized person. Dad would cook for me on a little camp stove when I came to his room. We would talk as we had before, as one adult to another, but I wasn't an adult. I was a self-absorbed teenager. I complained bitterly about everything, and in my own pain and frustration, I wasn't fully conscious of the magnitude of the changes in Dad's life. He had gone from being a respected, wealthy, well-employed married man to being a recluse in a mud hovel in the middle of nowhere, living on the good graces of his resentful brother-in-law. All this he did to keep his promise to God to watch over Cihangir and me. I never heard him complain about his reduced circumstances or express regret or doubt about his decision. He was a marvelous example of resilience and integrity, but I didn't completely recognize it at the time. I was just glad he was there, ever constant.

There was a big family fight just days after we arrived. Dad told me he was going to enroll me in the local school. I didn't mind going to school; in fact, I ordinarily loved school. But somehow, enrolling me sounded so permanent. If he put me in school here, it would really mean we were actually intending to stay, and *that* thought was unbearable.

Mustafa, my new father, had different ideas.

"She doesn't need to go to school," he announced. "She'll go to work in the factory and help support herself. You have brought me three more mouths to feed, remember," he told Dad.

Dad straightened to his full, impressive height and faced Mustafa. I had never seen him look as strong and immovable as he did then, like a boulder tumbled down into the house from the distant mountains.

"Ayse is going to school. She will not work in the factory."

"She will," Mustafa insisted. "A girl doesn't need education. I'll take her to the factory tomorrow."

"Absolutely not," Dad replied calmly. "You will have to walk over my dead body first."

The fight raged for a couple of days, and then a surprising thing happened. Fatma actually took Dad's side. She was a janitor at the primary school, and even though she hadn't received much education herself, she valued it and wanted her children to receive schooling. I don't know if she had ever in her life put her foot down before, but she did that time. She didn't raise her voice, but she looked Mustafa in the eye and said very firmly, "Ayse will go to school."

And so I did.

* * *

Even though Dad no longer worked, every day he would get dressed as if he were going to the factory, with his suit and necktie. The only time he didn't wear his tie was the weekend. He would read his newspaper and listen to music in his back room and hardly mix with the others in the family. However, every morning we children would all line up, youngest to oldest, and Dad would hand out an allowance, a few little coins to each child. He believed all of us should be treated equally and we all should have the opportunity to buy what we needed. He had his pension, but he spent most of it on us children.

Dad would go downtown every day to some favorite places of his to spend the day with the few friends he made, particularly a watchmaker he knew, a gentle and peaceful man who matched my father's temperament well. They would talk for hours every day, seated at the man's workbench while he repaired and built watches and clocks. At evening prayer, Dad would come home bearing scraps of meat for the cats. Every neighborhood cat knew when to expect him, and by the time he rounded our corner, he had twenty cats following him. He always told me, "Always feed others before you feed yourself." This is still my motto, and I'm always the last person to eat when I'm serving dinner.

The one time I asked Dad if he missed all the things we'd had in Istanbul, he replied, "It isn't good to have too many worldly things. We don't need very much. If it were up to me, I would like to cook our food in a pot and serve it on the lid." He always felt other people needed things more than he did, and he would forego purchases or give away what he had to make others more comfortable.

Even though Fatma and Mustafa were comparatively well off compared to some of their neighbors, since both of them had jobs, I still scorned them for being uneducated and ill-mannered. They had never seen the things I had seen and had not lived the life I had lived. Humility was not my strong point.

Adolescence is a difficult enough time anyway, a time of forming an identity separate from one's parents. But when one's parents turn out to be completely different people from what one had thought, it can be disorienting, and I made the whole intolerable situation worse. I nursed my anger and raised it into a wild, living thing. I didn't hide my dislike for my siblings. I couldn't help resenting the fact that my parents had kept three of their children and given two of us away. I didn't care that they had been poor, that perhaps they had seen it as the best thing for us to be raised far away. It was beside the point that I was glad I had been raised in Istanbul and not here in Karaman. I couldn't forgive what they had done. I felt powerless, and I lashed out at them in the only way I had available to me: by withholding love and respect from them.

Cihangir adapted quickly to life in Karaman because he was young. He got along fairly well with our parents. He was included in games with our new brothers as if it was the most natural thing in the world, and he seemed to like their company. As Dad had said, Cihangir had endured more of my mother than I had because I had been away at school. He seemed to find a sort of freedom here in this little village, out from under Mother's shadow, and didn't appear to miss Istanbul at all, which made me resent him a bit. Sometimes the other children would laugh behind their hands at my speech. I saw Cihangir's courtesy toward them as betrayal.

I hated my new siblings as much as I did my parents. I hated everything about them. The way they talked. The way they ate. How they did not brush their teeth. How they slept on the floor in a tangle like a litter of puppies. How they stood too closely while speaking to me. The list was endless in my mind.

The oldest was Mehmet. Like his father, he was fairly tall and thin, with dark hair and eyes. He didn't like school and often rebelled, refusing to attend, as his father had. Mustafa never insisted he go and, in fact, often encouraged him to seek employment instead of education. Mehmet and I did not get along well at all. He didn't like me either, seeing me as an arrogant intruder, and he made sure I knew about it. We constantly fought about many things. When he realized I liked school and was far superior in my language skills, he resentfully began destroying the few personal belongings I had begun to acquire.

I had been given a small number of old photographs of my early childhood. I kept these in an envelope under my sleeping mat and treasured them. They seemed to me to be a tenuous link to some sort of roots, a tiny anchor amidst the chaos. I would look at them in secret and tell myself *this* was who I was, and I would try to fit myself into the story they represented. One day after a fierce argument with me, Mehmet set fire to my envelope and destroyed all the photos. He had no idea how important those precious few photos had been to me . . . or perhaps he did, and that was why he targeted them. I came into the room to find a little pile of ashes sitting neatly beside my pillow. I could tell instantly what he had burned by the tiny corner bits that were left. I knelt beside the pitiful remains overcome with sorrow.

Behind me in the doorway, Mehmet laughed.

"How could you do that?" I screamed. "Those were all I had."

My devastation was instantly replaced with sheer rage. Oh, how I wanted him dead. I didn't care if I was arrested for it; I was going to kill him. I jumped to my feet and launched myself at him, and the smile vanished from his face. He could tell I was serious. Mehmet dodged my claws and stumbled backward into the front room, with me following right behind him.

"I am going to kill you," I shrieked. "I want you *gone*."

Without hesitation, I snatched up a knife from a tray and flung it at him, but he was too quick. He darted outside and closed the thick wooden door just as the knife struck it. The knife embedded itself in the wood where his face would have been and stuck there, quivering. I fell to my knees, bowed my forehead to the dirt floor, my arms wrapped around my stomach, and wept uncontrollably. It was several hours before Mehmet dared return home. It was certainly a good thing he escaped alive, but I admitted, even many years later, that I still had ill feelings about that terrible event in my life, and I still wished I had those photos of my childhood.

My younger brother Mustafa was kinder and gentler. He enjoyed going to school, so we had at least that in common. He struggled with his schoolwork, though, and when I offered, he allowed me to help him study. With the extra assistance, he managed to get good marks, which made him happy, and that made him feel more kindly toward me. Even though we had some things in common, though, most of the time we didn't share a common vision of life. He loved playing; I loved reading. He loved his parents; I despised them. We were total opposites of each other in that regard.

Though I didn't like how Cihangir seemed to slot himself effortlessly into our new life, I was always there to protect and defend him against our other siblings. He was too little to defend himself. He did enjoy playing with Mustafa, but whenever there was a disagreement, his two older brothers would unite against him. Having me on Cihangir's side helped even the battlefield. I made a promise many years ago that as long as I lived, I would continue to be a mother figure in his life.

My only sister was Hatice. There were eight years between us, and she was too young to be part of that "us" and "them" mentality. She didn't tend to choose sides in the fights unless her brothers bullied her into it. She was a beautiful little girl and tended to be jealous of her mother's attention, trying to secure a good place for herself in Fatma's life. She wasn't sure she wanted to share her mother with these two new strangers, of whose existence she hadn't even been aware before. As far as I was concerned, I was no threat—she could keep Fatma; I didn't want her to be my mother.

The other children would stick to themselves and exclude me, the way a herd of animals will distance themselves from a wounded or ill member of the group, leaving it vulnerable and unprotected. I sensed how such a rejected, wounded animal would feel, left to fight alone against any predator. I felt alone most of the time. When fights or arguments arose among us, though, I was glad to see Cihangir always took my side. Teams chosen, we would have violent gang wars, hot and fierce, with no rules. None of the adults seemed to care or attempted to stop us. Maybe they just realized it was hopeless. Maybe they were afraid to get caught in the middle, standing between two warring packs of hyenas. Cihangir never had as close a relationship with Dad as I did; it was me he came to whenever he was hurt or upset. But as soon as fights were over and games were on again, back he would go to the enemy's side, and I'd be alone once more.

My one dress I'd brought with me was too fine and nice, and it angered the others, who thought I felt myself above them (they were right, of course). Chin up, I wore that dress as much as possible until it practically fell to pieces. Any other cloth Fatma tried to give me felt scratchy and foreign and smelled funny. I looked down my nose at the homely and rustic and remembered the fine clothes Mother had bought me on our shopping sprees in Istanbul. What had she done with my closetful of clothing? Was it still hanging there, waiting for me to return and claim it? Had she thrown it all out the window after the trash can?

Looking back on it, I think the two years I spent in Karaman were more terrible and traumatic than the abusive years with Mother because everything was so intense. If Dad had not been there in the back room to run to, I would not have been able to endure my new life.

* * *

While Cihangir attended the run-down primary school near our home, I attended the run-down secondary school in another area. Such a sorry-looking building it was. I had thought the school in Besiktas was cheerless, but the school in Karaman couldn't even begin to compare. The gray concrete walls were ugly and dull. The classes were crowded with students my age, but nobody was like me. It was such a far cry from the posh private school I had attended, and I hated it. Still, it was something, and I went. I wanted an education, no matter how it came. The school reminded me of a hospital, with grayish white walls and long, dark hallways. Sometimes the classrooms were icy cold. The coal-heated furnace never gave enough heat during the long, bitter winter. We would huddle at the old desks, and when the other children pressed up against me on each side, I didn't push them away, even though I disliked them all, because it was the only way to keep warm. At times we would sit in class with our coats on.

It was strictly no-nonsense at this school: math and reading and writing, English, and a little bit of history and geography. The school budget did not allow for many extracurricular activities. There was certainly no music appreciation, no art or dancing, nothing to stimulate the imagination or bring beauty into life. The marching band was basically the only frill offered. This drabness perfectly reflected the bleakness I felt inside. Indeed, I would have been astonished to find anything beautiful in Karaman.

The other students tended to avoid me, and admittedly, I did little to encourage any friendships. But one ray of light in the darkness came

from an unexpected source; I loved my teachers. Even though the
school itself was depressing, the teachers were very kind to me. Perhaps
they sensed how miserable I was, how lost and foreign I felt. Thanks to
their efforts, my knowledge of the world expanded. I had a great desire
to learn new things, especially a new language. My love of English
started in grade seven. The curator of the local museum spoke English
and was also our classroom English teacher. He was one of the most
kind, compassionate men I knew. I adored him. I felt he understood
me because he was from a big city himself. I followed him around like
a shadow.

"*Hocam*, how do you say this in English? How do you say that?" I
would ask. He was always very patient and took the time to teach me new
words.

"Hello, Ayse. How are you today?" he would ask politely in English.

"I am fine, thank you. And you?" I would reply back proudly.

I loved the way he spoke. English was beautiful coming from his
mouth. I liked everything about him. I loved his mannerisms and how
he dressed, and I wondered how he had ever ended up in such a town
as this. He was my ideal of what higher education looked like. He
made a big impact on me, and I promised myself I would master the
English language one day and become like him.

* * *

Long gone were the days of keeping silent. I no longer cried quietly
to myself but let everyone around me know my emotions—and the
emotion I felt most often was anger. I learned to raise my voice, all right.
I was a free-spirited person and wouldn't bow to anyone. My biological
family must have felt like a jaguar had been dropped into their laps.

Fatma would become frustrated with my resistance and disobedience
and would try to beat me, the only solution she knew. It had worked
with her other children, for the most part. But when she hit me, I
would hit her back, an unthinkable thing in that community. I could
stand up to her in ways I could never have stood up to Turkan because
she did not wield the power over me that Turkan had. After a few
times, Fatma learned physical abuse would not be a successful way to
deal with me. We didn't understand each other or even try to. I had
no interest in getting to know her. In her eyes, she was the mother and

whatever she said was law. She couldn't understand that I didn't view her as my mother at all. She had given up any right to parent me as far as I was concerned. If she raged, I raged back.

Most of all, I disliked her because she said I didn't need two fathers. She and Mustafa didn't like having Dad live in the mud hut behind the house, whether because of his former high position and wealth or because they found his quiet presence smothering, I don't know. Perhaps they felt he was judging the way they lived or criticizing their parenting, though I rarely saw evidence of this. He was always respectful and polite and tried not to interfere more than necessary in anything unless it directly impacted Cihangir or me, although he could be immovable when he disagreed with something. Whatever the reason, they resented him, and fights with him were frequent. My father Mustafa wanted my dad to go away.

But Dad refused to go. He simply said, "These are my children, and you will have to step over my dead body to get them. I will never forsake them. I only brought them back because legally I had to, but they are mine." They kept hoping he would leave, but he never did until the day he died in that little hut in 1982.

Chapter Eight

"The burden of the desert of the sea. As whirlwinds in the south pass through; so it cometh from the desert, from a terrible land."
—Isaiah 21:1

AT THE TIME OF OUR arrival in Karaman, everything seemed to me to be the same color—dusty gold brown, the color of stone, the color of dirt. *Barren* was the only word to describe it. I never felt completely clean. The dust blew in the air and became grit between my teeth. The sun drew the moisture out of my skin until I felt as dusty as the street, and my hair would crackle with static when I brushed it. I was surrounded by brown, all shades of brown, and gray stone, without relief. I longed for the garden of my old boarding school, for the color of apricots and rich red carpets, for the multicolored clothing of my former classmates. I missed the shelter of my beloved willow tree. There had once been a lot of trees in Karaman, I was told, but people had plundered them and used them for wood and building material. I wished they had kept at least a few of the trees to break up the color of the place, if for nothing else. I craved shade and coolness and water.

There was electricity and water available where we lived but not in every household. Many homes still had outhouses instead of indoor plumbing. The main road led into our neighborhood and then abruptly ended, as if giving up in despair of ever reaching anywhere else, and after that, it was just stones.

Just as I was thinking Karaman was the end of the world for me, my parents took me to visit my actual birthplace, Cukurbag, several miles away. This littlest of little villages was beyond belief. There was no road, no electricity, and little transportation. The minibus from Karaman came only once a day, so visitors had to sleep in Cukurbag overnight. The only main dirt road ended at the entrance to the village. Compared to Cukurbag, even I had to admit Karaman was light-years ahead. The miserable stone-and-mud hut where I had been born was a shock to me. And to think that I had been appalled that Jesus had been born in a humble stable. What do you know—so had I.

Cukurbag sat in a basin. The hills surrounding it were hard gray rock, jutting up in rough peaks, nearly impervious to explosives. During my visit, I let myself explore a little, looking for a way out if nothing else. I discovered that on three sides of the town, there were vineyards. The leaves of the vines seemed yellow and thirsty to me, but the grapes themselves were admittedly beautiful and—when I helped myself to some—tasted wonderful. The name of the village meant "a vineyard in a ditch." There was farmland as far as the eye could see around the town. I was surprised to see that the dirt ranged in color from black to brown to orange. Dad later told me the orange was from the iron content.

Fatma's mother, Hatice, lived in Cukurbag in a two-room stone house. One room was to sleep in, the other to cook in. She was a grouchy looking woman who frightened me at first, but beneath the tough exterior, I found a soft heart. Like Fatma, she was quiet and didn't mix with people much. Unless she had something nice to say, she wouldn't say anything. She knew the whole story about Cihangir and me, and she put great effort into making me comfortable. She took pains to make foods I liked, and she stroked my hair. She talked to me as if my opinion mattered. She had married at the age of fifteen and had a good way with children that soothed me. I found I could confide in her somewhat, and she would counsel me to be patient with the challenges in my life, knowing that things weren't going to come easily for me. She was very different from Turkan's and Mustafa's mother, Havva, who lived in Karaman.

Havva was a real character, a unique woman, and fast on her feet. If needed, she would beg, borrow, and steal in order to feed anyone who came to her home—any means justifying the resulting hospitality. She was also a chatterbox, the words streaming from her mouth like water from a pitcher (I've been told I resemble her in this regard).

Grandmother Havva worked hard all her life and was very industrious. She had no patience for those who did not work, and she had little to do with her son Omer, who skirted around employment the way I dodged goat dung in the road. Firm and stubborn in her opinions, Havva either loved or hated, with nothing lukewarm in between. She had lived in Cukurbag most of her life but had eventually moved to Karaman. She had been very young when she'd had the affair and given birth to Turkan out of wedlock, and this had been followed by nine marriages (some of which were legal and some of which were not, being religious marriages only and not civil). Whenever she lost one husband, through death or divorce, her children would tell her it was not good for a Muslim woman to die as a single woman and that she should find another man to marry who could protect her and take care of her. Personally, I thought they said this so she would find someone else to look after her so they could be rid of her.

Grandmother Havva never tolerated abuse or defiance, and she was extremely independent. She and her husband were each responsible for paying their own bills. One day her (then current) husband told her, "You're eating too much. It's too expensive."

Grandmother replied, "Well, you're burning the lights too much. That's too expensive too."

This turned into a heated argument, and her husband tapped her a few times on the back of the hand with a small metal rod as a sort of punishment. Grandmother was furious at this and left the house, slamming the door behind her. She came to Mustafa's house and told him what had happened. She was affronted that her husband had scolded her like an unruly schoolchild.

Mustafa went to Grandmother's husband and told him, "My mother really loves you and would like to make up with you. Here's what you do: why don't you buy some fruit and other goodies and bring them to our house and make up with her?"

Pleased that she wanted his forgiveness, Grandmother's husband thought this was a good idea, so he came to our house with the bag of fruit and other offerings. When he arrived, the rest of us were waiting outside for him, but Grandmother was waiting alone in the house. He gave us all a polite nod and took off his shoes, as was customary, before entering the home. Mustafa let him enter the house first, but instead of coming in after him, he closed the door and locked it, and the man was locked in the room with Grandmother Havva. Grandmother was waiting with a stick, and she beat her husband soundly. We were all standing outside the door listening to him yell: "Open up. I can't get out. Unlock the door!" We could hear the slaps and thuds as Grandmother's stick found its mark.

When Mustafa finally unlocked the door, Grandmother's husband burst out, wild-eyed, bloody-nosed, and hair on end. He took off running up the lane.

"You forgot your shoes," Mustafa called after him helpfully.

"I don't want your mother, and I don't want the shoes! You can keep them," Grandmother's husband called back over his shoulder as he kept running.

Grandmother Havva came out of the house, propped her stick against the wall, and brushed her hands together, a smug look on her face, as if she'd just had a very satisfying meal. I've never laughed as hard as I did that day. A short time later, Grandmother and her husband were divorced. No, Grandmother never was one to tolerate nonsense.

In spite of her fierceness, Grandmother Havva was especially tolerant of children. There was a gentle humanity hidden beneath her prickly exterior. My brothers would give her wine and tell her it was cough medicine. They liked to see her get dizzy and silly. Or when she was praying, they would sneak up behind her and pin her skirt to her prayer mat with safety pins without her noticing. When she tried to stand, she wouldn't be able to because she was pinned fast to the carpet. The boys would giggle like crazy, but Grandmother only waved her cane at them and never hit them.

I have a particularly fond spot in my heart for Grandmother Havva. Her toughness, independence, and undying optimism have been an example to me. I like to think I have inherited some of her feistiness.

* * *

When winter came to Karaman, it was very cold, and my lips and the skin on my hands dried and cracked. From somewhere, Dad managed to find us coats, a bit small but serviceable. I found it very trying, living in the little house in Karaman with no heat but what came from the stove or each other's bodies. In spite of the cold, I couldn't stand being in the little house for long. I chafed to be outdoors and away from the crowded room. I would walk as far as the edge of town, hands pushed into my pockets and shoulders hunched, and stand staring down the road toward the north, imagining myself back home. But it was too cold to stay for long, and I would sadly turn back to the house with a feeling of lead in my heart.

Spring was a relief and a gift because all those shades of brown slowly turned into shades of green, all kinds of green. Wildflower seeds blew in from every direction and bloomed wherever they fell, changing the hue of the landscape to purple, white, and red. It was an actual physical comfort to see something besides brown, brown, and brown. Spring made me think that perhaps God was merciful after all.

Dad and I walked through the fields sometimes, as we had walked the streets of Istanbul. He told me the colors of the wildflowers were different every year, depending on what seeds happened to blow in. In May I was delighted when the field across from the house broke out all over with big red poppies, popping up like a surprise party. I soaked up those vibrant colors, storing them in my mind because I knew they wouldn't last. In three weeks' time, they had disappeared.

All my life I had loved animals, but, of course, with Mother's germ phobia, no pets had been allowed. Now I was surrounded by them. Young boys herded goats through the streets. Many people kept chickens that ran in and out of their homes as freely as the people did. There were stray dogs and feral cats everywhere.

Fatma had a domesticated house cat that liked popcorn and olives. It would hurry to be the first to the table if one of those two things was being served. There it would sit, daintily eating olives and spitting out the pits. Our first spring in Karaman, the cat gave birth to five kittens, the cutest things I'd ever seen. But the mother cat was not a very good mother and always found ways to get out of the house and desert her babies. Dad observed her for a few days and was concerned that the kittens would starve. This worried me as well.

"We have to do something. Can't you force her to stay with her kittens?" I wailed.

"I don't know if you can force a bad mother to be a good one," Dad replied, but he agreed to try to help.

One day Dad caught the mother cat by the scruff of the neck as she tried to make her escape again. He held her up in front of him and waved a flyswatter threateningly in her face. He didn't hit her, but the implication was clear: if she didn't take better care of her kittens, he'd beat her. The cat froze, staring at Dad with wide yellow eyes, and I could tell she knew he wasn't kidding.

The next day, the mother cat was about to take off out the door again, and Dad picked up the flyswatter and raised it. The cat spun back around, ran back to her kittens, and assumed the position to nurse them. The look on her face made me laugh.

"It just goes to show you," Dad mused, "a little discipline goes a long way, even for cats."

Summer followed spring with shades of yellow, and it was unbearably hot. There was little rain, and the land around Karaman became scorched. Men carried great baskets of beans, wheat, sugar beets, and onions into the market. In September, there were the grapes again, and the heat let up a little. Fall was the best time of year.

As my first year in Karaman stretched into two and I entered my early teens, I began to visit Cukurbag more often (perhaps because the contrast between it and Karaman made me feel better about living there). I admit I started to enjoy these visits. As the village moved through its own procession of colors, there was a parade of smells as well. As I approached the outskirts of the town, I would be greeted by the stench of manure. Especially in the evening, when they came back from the fields, all the animals, as if in a united chorus announced, "We're back," and no one could miss it. Other smells differed with the seasons. In the spring, there was the fresh smell of the newborn goats. Then the sheep and calves arrived. Some people owned baby donkeys and horses, and the animals all cried at different levels.

In Cukurbag, villagers had a small piece of land, undifferentiated from their neighbor's by any sort of visible border, but the boundaries were nonetheless well understood. There they planted beans, corn, onions, and other staples. The villagers would gather everything grown in Cukurbag, deduct what they were going to eat, and then take the surplus into Karaman to sell. With their small earnings they bought salt, lamp oil, and soap. It was my first experience really watching commerce in action. In my grandmother's day, they'd used donkeys to take the produce to the city, but gradually, they had switched to using trucks. There was an ancient minibus that carried passengers between the marketplace and our area. The bus driver slept in the village overnight and made the return trip to the city the next day. That was it—just the one bus. I would watch it drive away and wish I could go with it. I dreamt of returning to Istanbul.

After observing matters for a while, I once suggested that the villagers in Cukurbag collectively plant their crops rather than each family having their own tiny plot. If they pooled together to bring a bigger product to market, they would then be able to negotiate better prices and bigger profits. They could collectively be pitted against rivals in Karaman rather than competing amongst themselves for their share of the market. To my mind, it made perfect and obvious sense. But they said that wasn't the way their grandfathers had done it, so they weren't going to change. That surprised me, to learn that people didn't want to change. I felt like I had changed regularly and often all my life; why couldn't they?

I can only describe that place now with an adult's perspective because I didn't grow up there. I was always the outsider. Everybody in the village knew everybody else and was, more often than not, related to each other. There were perhaps two hundred people at most in Cukurbag, and most of them were older adults. The younger generation tended to move away.

In one of our talks in his little back room, Dad told me that half of Cukurbag and many from Karaman had moved to Germany, France, Holland, or Belgium as workers in the 1960s. They had raised their children and grandchildren there, and then some of them had come back.

"I can't for the life of me imagine why they would," I declared. "If ever I can get away from this place, I'll never return."

Dad just looked at me patiently a moment and then said, "If one day your life takes you back to Istanbul or even farther, Ayse, a part of you will still be here, whether you like it or not. You can't get away from who you are."

"This isn't who I am."

He smiled. "Who are you, then?"

"I don't know yet, but I'll find out. And when I do, it won't be here in Karaman."

"You can be a good citizen no matter where you live," he replied peacefully.

"Maybe so," I answered. "But I'll go be a good citizen somewhere else." Under my breath I added, "Anywhere else."

* * *

Once in a while we would see Omer, who had a run-down, miserable mud house in Karaman. He was married now to a rather slow-minded woman and had four children—three girls and a boy. The boy's name was Necmi, after my father, and one of the girls was named Turkan. Omer was very abusive to his wife, and she eventually divorced him. Omer ended up with custody of the four children. He was a very giving and caring person, and I know he tried his best to be a good father to his children, who loved him deeply, but his drinking was out of control, to the point that he would drink gasoline for its alcohol content. Now and then he would halfheartedly find work in construction, but he tended to work one hour and then nap for two, so the companies would let him go. As Cihangir grew older, he became friends with Omer, and sometimes they would work—and be fired—together. Omer still relied primarily on my mother Turkan for financial support, and she in turn relied on my father.

There was a mosque right next to our home in Karaman. It was nothing to compare to Istanbul's Blue Mosque, of course, but was just as important to the town as the Blue Mosque was to Istanbul. Our mosque was a one-room concrete building with a short minaret, and inside were small, donated prayer rugs covering the floor in a patchwork of reds and oranges. Back in Istanbul, I had used the Mosque as orientation, my reference point for getting around the city. In Karaman, there was no danger of getting lost. It was like living in a tiny-scale model of a place—a toy town, not real to me at all.

The mosque was the center of life. Shoes were left at the door. Only men went to the mosque except for the month of Ramadan. After the last call of prayer during Ramadan, women could go to the mosque to read the Koran and pray, but they stayed in a segregated area with their heads covered. In the summer there were religious courses offered to both boys and girls, who were allowed to mix until they reached puberty.

Anyone getting married or buried had to go through the mosque at least once. I quickly learned everything was a community affair. There was no such thing as privacy. All was communal. People worked together, married together, played, cried, prayed, and buried together. If you didn't, you were shunned. There was no such thing as living in privacy. It just wasn't done. It took me awhile to get used to the idea that people would just knock and walk right into the house without waiting to be invited and that everyone felt entitled to know everyone else's business.

Whatever they cooked, they shared, no questions asked. Especially in the summer, there were a lot of weddings and therefore a lot of cooking. Everyone brought *big* pots the size of laundry tubs, and it was all very noisy. I could smell burnt fat and onions all the time through the streets. People talked as they cooked and ate together, and I stood on the fringes, watching and listening but not participating. A lot of the talk was gossip about the neighbors. Some of the talk was about the lack of rain. The elders in the neighborhood said the rain was withheld because of the wicked younger generation not doing the right things and not living righteously. I listened and felt they were talking about me, blaming me and my sins for the drought. There were a lot of prayers for rain.

Dad accepted his new circumstances in life with quiet dignity. Cihangir cheerfully fit into his new home and family and left the past behind.

I made plans for my escape.

Chapter Nine

"Study and learn, and become acquainted with all good books."
—Doctrine and Covenants 90:15

As BEST AS I CAN guess, I think I was born in about 1963, but my birth wasn't registered until about two years later. People who registered late had to pay a fine, and, of course, Mustafa didn't have the means to do that, so he hid my birth by registering me under a relative's name. People didn't pay much attention to details like age, so I don't know to this day exactly how old I am. When I sat down to figure it out for the purposes of this book, I spent twenty minutes scribbling out a time line on paper and finally gave up. The only anchors I have are these: I know I spent five years at the boarding school as a child. I remember the Turks invading Cyprus in 1974 when we were living in Besiktas. And I know I finished eighth grade in Karaman in 1976.

I wanted to take the high school entrance exam, but I was told I was too young. I would have been thirteen . . . perhaps. In any case, I have never been good at backing down or accepting situations that displeased me. I took matters in hand, went to court (along with two paid witnesses), and had it officially declared that I was born in 1960 and was therefore sixteen. Ta da! I was old enough to take the exam.

One afternoon I went into Dad's back room to speak to him. He was cutting onions on a little board, preparing for supper. He took one look at my face and knew something was up. He set the knife aside and just waited, one eyebrow cocked.

I knew there was no point in making small talk first. I got right to the point.

"I want to attend teacher's college."

This was the equivalent of high school, except students came out of it with a certificate that qualified them to teach. It was a boarding school, paid for by the government, so cost was not an issue.

"I see. That is good, Ayse. It's a good goal to have. There will be an examination."

"I already took the entrance exam," I told him. I had taken it without my family's knowledge.

Dad thought about this a moment and then asked quietly, "Don't your parents have to sign the papers?"

"I forged their signatures," I said stoutly. I kept my eyes firmly on his, refusing to look away.

Dad didn't remark on that comment. Instead he said, "Have you been accepted?"

"Not yet, but I will be. I haven't told anyone else yet. But I'm determined to go."

He looked at me a little longer and then returned to his onions. "You do what you have to do," was all he said.

When I received word that I had been accepted to teacher's college, I went home and announced to everyone that I was going to school in Konya, a hundred kilometers to the north. This news was met with stony silence from my parents. I could feel the disapproval radiating off them. But perhaps they were also partly relieved to see this troublesome teenager go. I packed up and went, and I felt as if I were running away from home . . . which I suppose I was.

At registration the first day, Dad came with me on the rickety bus and signed himself as my father. Nobody asked if he was really my father or not. They just accepted it. Our last names were different, but nobody said anything. I was exhilarated to finally be away from Karaman. We said good-bye, and this time it wasn't as dramatic as our first good-bye when I was six/four/nine. I was glad to be there. I think Dad was also pleased that I had this opportunity.

* * *

The three years I spent at the school in Konya were the best years of my life to that point. Konya was a lovely city of red roofs and minarets and domes. Mine was an all-girls secular boarding school, and wearing the head covering was forbidden. That was fine with me. I had never adopted Fatma's custom of covering her head. I immediately set about making friends at my new school, determined that these years would be better than the past few had been.

I had much in common with one of the girls I knew there, Pelin Ercan, and she instantly became my friend and remains my friend to this day. In fact, she felt more like a sister to me than a friend. She was smart, kind, and loving, and was one of the few people who respectfully valued my opinion. I had never experienced that before from anyone but Dad. Respect. I felt good around her.

As much as I loved my life in Konya, life on the weekends was difficult for me. Many of the parents came to visit their daughters. Nobody came to visit me in Konya but Dad, who came on the bus every Saturday. He would bring food for picnics and interesting bits of news, just as he had when I was a child in boarding school.

I still had no contact with Turkan, though she had kept writing letters to Dad over the years, asking him to come back to her or to send her money. (He never replied, though he did send money, and he kept the letters, which I have now.) Of course, my biological parents never visited me, nor did I expect or want them to. I would have been astonished if they had.

I met wonderful teachers who influenced me for life, especially my music teacher. Music became my passion, and I studied hard and was consistently on the honor roll. I followed my teacher around as she watered her plants. Some days she would ask me to help her. I loved that menial task. The green leaves and bright flowers were like a breath of fresh air in my mundane life. I loved watching the filtered sunlight dance on the bright flowers. I made myself a promise at that time that if I ever had a house of my own, I would fill it with real, living plants and flowers. I was always making promises to myself about the future and what it would be like. For the most part, they have come true.

Our dorms were two classrooms that held thirty rows of two-layered bunk beds. We had tiny metal lockers, and everything we owned in the world went into those lockers. There were only a few wealthy kids in the school—it wasn't a private school—so most of the students were from humble origins like me. I couldn't help thinking how my terms of reference had changed. I had attended the boarding school in Istanbul as the pampered only daughter of a wealthy chemical engineer. Now I was in Konya as one of the five children of an illiterate laborer from Karaman. I fiercely told myself I would disregard where or how I had originated. I would be *me*, whatever I chose to make of myself, independent of anything or anyone else. I would create the person I wanted to be and make that identity my reality.

I quickly settled into the rigid routine of the school. I liked the predictability of the rules, the reliability of what was expected of me. There were no surprises, but that also meant no occasions for impulsiveness or spontaneity. We got up at five thirty when a teacher came in and abruptly turned on the lights. We had half an hour to dress and make our bunk beds, which had to be perfectly made like military cots. (I was finally tall enough to make mine without having to hop on my knees on the blankets.) The teachers would bounce coins off the blankets, and if they weren't tight enough, we had to make the bed again. At six the teacher came again to tell us to leave the dormitory, and it was locked. Heaven help you if you forgot something because you couldn't get back into the room until evening.

For one hour we had study time. We sat on hard benches at long tables and tried not to nod over our books. This was followed by exercising, which helped wake us up a bit. We had to do jumping jacks in the courtyard, rain or shine, for fifteen minutes. From seven fifteen to seven forty-five was breakfast. We were given bread and either powdered milk (which tasted nasty) or tea (which tasted equally nasty). Some days we would get three or four black olives and a tiny square of cheese the size of a coin, and on other days we would have margarine and jam. That's all there ever was, and there was no point in hoping for seconds or any kind of variety.

After breakfast the seven fifty bell would ring, and we had ten minutes to get ready for class. We had to be out of the halls by eight sharp, when the bell rang to start class. If ever a student was late, there was trouble. The hall monitor would take the poor girl by the ear and haul her to the class, which was embarrassing. I always made sure I was on time and prepared.

We had no electives. Everyone took the same classes until the second year, when we could either choose languages (verbal) or sciences. Still enamored of English, I chose verbal.

Promptly at noon, there was lunch. This consisted mainly of legumes, stones and all. I never wanted to be late because the last to the table would get the stones at the bottom of the pot. We ate from steel trays, and there was usually no knife because there was nothing that required cutting. We were never served meat except on special occasions, though I remember sometimes having ground beef or chunks of stew meat in something. But we never ate straight meat. We ate a lot of macaroni, rice, or bulgar and bread. We were given only water to drink in white ceramic jugs set out on the long tables. Usually we had fruit for dessert, nothing fancy but something sugary, such as dates. On Kurban Bayrami (our version of Eid) or other special occasions, those who stayed behind and didn't go home, including myself, got good meals: meat, vegetables, proper dessert, and candy.

After lunch, we were given a little free time to mingle in the yard. It was a rather dismal space—square, with cement paving and only a few benches and potted plants. We didn't have a lot of free time, but my friends and I made the most of it. With our imaginations, we could turn that dreary courtyard into anything or anyplace.

Of course, being in a school for girls, dating and boys weren't part of our lives, though we talked about such things now and then. One time an earthquake hit eastern Turkey, and seven boys were sent to board at our school because theirs had been destroyed. We had nothing to do with them though because they were from the east, and we didn't mingle with easterners. We certainly didn't date them because they might be Kurds. Many considered them unhandsome and beneath notice anyway.

The girls chatted a lot in the yard; there was always something to talk about and, frankly, little else to do in the empty yard. The turbulent political climate in Turkey trickled down to us in our isolated school, and we talked about Karl Marx's *Capital*, which we were reading. We memorized portions of the Communist Manifesto. Pelin and I loved to talk about current political events and how much we wanted to change the broken system. We formed a little group and enjoyed our like-minded discussions. We could talk and debate for hours. Time was irrelevant when we were wrapped up in a good conversation. Only our closeness and sisterhood mattered. Now, more than ever, I realize the value of our solid education in those years. It shaped my ideals and the political views I have today.

Dad wrote to me often, his letters providing happy intervals between his visits. And he always told me, "Be a good citizen and have faith in God," and "Love your country and defend those who cannot defend themselves." I always remembered his words. Our group came up with little manifestos of our own and became known as the Communists of the school. We girls became quite outspoken about any perceived inequality or injustice.

At one thirty, the bell rang, our debates had to end, and we were back in class until four. At that time, we had free time for two hours (which I usually spent reading or listening to music), followed by another study hour. At seven, we ate dinner (the same food as lunch, reheated). At eight thirty in the evening, the dorms were unlocked, and we hurried to get ready for bed. At nine sharp, the lights went off whether you were ready or not. The teacher would say, "Good night, everybody!" and turn off the switch, no exceptions or delays. That room of sixty girls was never completely quiet. Someone was always coughing or giggling, goofing around or stealing another girl's pillow. My friends and I would lie there in the dark and talk while other students yelled at us to go to sleep. I would sometimes hide under my covers and listen to music on my little battery-operated radio. Everyone knew I was doing it, but no one said anything.

Even though I settled into the routine, I disliked the early bedtime hour, and I promised myself that all my life I would go to bed late, as long as I lived, to make up for having to go to bed at nine. I still keep that promise to myself, and I get up very early as well as a leftover habit.

Saturday morning was "the bath." It was quite an event. Starting with the youngest students, everybody took turns, one class at a time, going to the bathhouse downstairs. The water had to be boiled in the big boiler tanks heated by wood and coal. Whoever got there first had good luck because the water was nice and warm. We had exactly half an hour to wash. There was nowhere to put our clothing, so we left our things behind and wore only a robe or towel into the bathhouse. There was no shower, only little marble tubs full of water. We would sit around the edge of the tub in groups of three or four and take turns dipping with plastic cups to pour water over ourselves. In this way, we sluiced off a piece of ourselves at a time, but we never submerged our whole bodies at once.

Shampoo was a luxury we didn't have. Only a few rich kids had shampoo, and once they realized everyone wanted to borrow it, they didn't bring it anymore. We used government-supplied soap, which had no scent and left behind a white residue like ashes. Whenever I used it, I thought of Turkan standing at the sink with her lovely white soap, turning it over and over in her hands. We had crocheted mitts our families provided to scrub with (someone gave me one because my family didn't crochet). The older students were last into the room, so the water was lukewarm or downright cold. Our teeth chattered as we huddled in our towels in that cold stone room. As we got older, we took shorter baths.

Saturdays and Sundays, when Dad visited me at school, there were times it was too cold to go out. And sometimes Dad had no money to take me out. But there was a visiting area where we could have a little picnic with the food he brought. It was a little like the visiting area of a jail. Dad was sometimes ill during my last year of school, so he missed two or three visits, but otherwise he always came. I knew I could rely on him, and he was my strength.

I didn't return to Karaman very often; there was no peace at home. I went back to visit a few times during the Muslim celebration of Eid, but because there was so much tension in the house, I didn't stay with my family. I would go to a friend's house instead. I had a couple of honorary or surrogate "mothers" who looked after me; my friend Pelin's mother, Pakize, was one of them. She always welcomed me into her poor but happy dwelling. There was always a place for me at their table, and though they didn't have much, they shared whatever they had. She loved me as if I were truly one of her children and made sure I received whatever her children received. I felt very special in her home. Not only she but all of her children welcomed me into their lives without question, and in time, I viewed them as my "real" family.

Pelin was the oldest daughter and a second mother to her siblings. She overcame many difficulties to make a better life for her family. Didar was the second daughter, a few years younger than us. She was a wonderful sister with many talents, a kind and caring little girl with a heart of gold. Filiz was the youngest daughter, with long, black hair and lovely dark eyes, and was very gentle, polite, and quiet. And there was Mehmet, the only male child, and the pride and joy of the whole family. He was a very smart and obedient boy. Oh, how much I loved this family and how much they loved me back! They were a balm to my soul.

Like me, Pelin definitely had her challenges. One day I found her crying in our bedroom at school. She had just received word that her beloved father had died. I remember that awful news as if it were yesterday. I put my arms around her, and she and I cried together for hours. I imagined how it would feel to lose my own father, and my heart ached for Pelin, Mother Pakize, and their family. The unknown scared both of us. Her poor mother. I felt her sorrow in my soul. Pakize was now a young widow with four young children. She had no money and no education. What was she to do? Where was she to go? I knew only too well the feeling of being misplaced in life.

When I visited home, Mustafa, proud of his lack of education, did not want me to talk about my experiences at school. He thought I was putting myself above everyone else, and my brothers emulated his attitude toward education. Unfortunately, even Cihangir thought I was foolish for going away to school and believed I should stay home and learn to run a household like a proper female. Fatma, standing in the middle of her tiny dirt house, was my unexpected ally when it came to education. It was probably the only thing she agreed on with my father and the only thing about which she stood up to Mustafa. I often talked about these differences and tensions with Dad, sitting on his bedroll in the little mud room, and he always encouraged me, saying, "This too shall pass."

Dad was a very wise man. He had the patience of a prophet and a sixth sense about life. It was not unusual for him to predict things that would happen. Often the things he said sounded like prophetic utterances, and I learned to trust them. Once he said that even if Turkan came to find him in the dark with a candle, he still wouldn't return to her. He continued to ignore her letters and telegrams that pled and threatened and begged for him to return. He knew she was provided for financially, and that was the extent of his obligation. He wanted no other contact.

Then one evening the power went out, and he and I were having dinner by candlelight. We heard a disturbance outside, and we looked up to see someone standing in the doorway. Mother had arrived in Karaman. It was just as Dad had spoken. She had come to find him in the dark with the light of a candle, and he did not go back to her.

Mother ignored me as I sat there stunned and immobile. I may as well not even have been in the room. She zeroed in on Dad immediately.

"I've come to take you back to Istanbul with me," she declared.

For a minute he froze, staring at her, and then Dad put down his fork and slowly rose to his feet to face her.

When he said nothing, she repeated loudly, "I've come to take you back with me."

"No, Turkan. I have told you already. I'm not coming back."

"I came all this way to get you." She gestured with her arms as she spoke, and the scarves at her waist fluttered like little flags on a battleship.

"You shouldn't have come. It was pointless."

"But you are my husband. You have to look after me."

"No. I have given you enough money to live on. That is the extent of my obligation to you. I can't live with all that again, Turkan."

She began to scream and wail. Dad continued to repeat that he would do nothing more for her. Mustafa appeared in the yard behind her and tried to quiet Mother. A small number of our neighbors gathered. It was like my childhood all over again, the lights coming on and the neighbors listening to all that went on in our house. Something inside me wanted to shrink and cower, but my new, angrier self stepped forward.

"Dad," I said over the sound of her tirade, "please stop arguing with her. Can't you see she is upset and talking nonsense as usual?"

Dad ran his hands down his face, looking very tired. But being a kind man, he agreed not to yell at her or continue the argument. Fatma and a neighbor woman managed to get Mother into the house. Dad and I sat in the light of the sputtering candle and listened to her sobs and obscenities next door. Eventually Mother wound down, and all fell quiet. I looked at Dad, and he looked bleakly at me.

"At least," he said quietly, "there are no dishes or mirrors to break here."

I couldn't help wanting to laugh, but the grief on his face stopped me. We listened to Fatma and Mustafa trying to reason with Mother next door.

She finally agreed to leave without further protest. She went back to Istanbul, and for several years, we didn't see her or hear a single word from her. Years later, when I was away at university, she suddenly reappeared and moved into a small house in Karaman. A neighbor told us she had rented a place not far from where Dad lived. Dad still refused to see her. It was only then that I appreciated the depth of the misery he had suffered with her, the extent of his pain through those years in Istanbul. He had run interference for Cihangir and me and had taken the brunt of her illness. But he would take no more.

Chapter Ten

*"Cease from anger, and forsake wrath: fret
not thyself in any wise to do evil."*
—*Psalm 37:8*

PELIN, AS ALWAYS, CONTINUED TO invite me to her house at every opportunity. She and I loved to read the classics, especially Kafka, Dostoevsky, and the Brontës. We talked incessantly about what we read. Pelin and I went through every difficulty at school together. It makes a difference when you have comradery. It was a new experience for me; it was warming to have a close friend other than my father.

We studied hard with a friendly competition because we knew right from the beginning that education was the key to breaking poverty. I was the class president and music club president, and later I became student body president. I kept very involved in student life.

On weekends, we students were free to go into town and roam around on our own. We could go on Saturday or Sunday but not both. Konya was a small town, but there were things to do. While the other girls went to restaurants or stores, Pelin and I went into the jails to support the left-wing activists. We took them food, medicine, and cigarettes. The guards would say, "You have nothing better to do than visit these Communists?" It was all very hush-hush, of course. If the school had found out, we would have been kept from going into town.

We were not afraid of anything, and we felt that being young gave us the right to challenge authority. The political turmoil in the country was affecting all of us. Life was becoming more and more challenging for most of us, especially for the working poor. Unemployment had risen to about 25 percent. The devaluation of the Turkish lira meant deep cuts at every level, including the Ministry of Education. Things were getting so worrisome that our principal was compelled to talk to us in a general assembly. We were called into the gymnasium, and the principal stood to address us. With his words, our world turned upside down.

"I realize when you first entered this school it was with the understanding that it was a four-year program with a diploma at the end and you would be entitled to teach when you graduated."

We all looked at each other, wondering what was coming. The principal coughed and continued quickly.

"The government has announced that going forward, they are dropping the fourth year and turning this school into a regular high school. This will be your last year here."

"But what about our teaching certificates?" someone called out.

"They will not be issued. You are no longer in a teaching program."

I was stunned. My plans were ruined. If I wasn't going to teach after all this, what was I going to do? I certainly couldn't go back to Karaman.

"They can't do this," Pelin hissed. "How can they just decide arbitrarily to do this to us?"

"Without any warning," added someone else.

"We can't let them. We entered this school with an understanding. It was an *agreement*," I protested.

"What can we do?" Pelin asked, spreading her hands.

"We have to tell the government we're not going to accept this," I said. "We have to make them hear us."

"How? Will they listen to us?"

I thought about the manifestos we had concocted, the ideals I had read about—how, theoretically, Communism put the power into the hands of the people. When would there be a better time to put it to the test?

"We're going to boycott," I declared.

And so the Great Boycott was born.

We got a group of students together and determined we would make the government hear our voice. We had great expectations of how we could influence them and change things according to our own will. We used our free time in Konya to buy black paint and brushes, which we smuggled into the school. One night after everyone was in bed, we took our white bedsheets, ripped them in half, sewed them into a huge banner, and painted on it "There is a boycott in the school." (At the time, it seemed brilliant to us.)

We went up to the balcony on the roof and hung the banner down the wall, where all would see it as they came to breakfast in the morning.

It caused quite a reaction. People gathered to look. Someone called the media, and they came to the gates to take pictures. The principal came out and looked at the sign then turned to look at the crowd of students and demanded to know who the culprits were. Pelin and I and a few others stepped proudly forward.

"We are the ones," I said.

"You think you're going to change the entire system by writing this on the wall?" he asked.

We were adamant. "We have to stand against this and make the school go back to the way it was," we argued. "They can't destroy all our plans, our future."

He only shook his head and went back inside. We began our campaign in earnest.

"Don't go to lunch. Don't go to classes," we urged the other students as they crossed the courtyard. "We have to show the government we don't want them involved in our lives. Our futures should be our choice."

At first the boycott was a great success in our eyes. Many people, more than we had hoped, chose to boycott lunch and classes. People heard about the uproar and came to watch from outside the gates. We had a glorious time shouting our slogans. Of course, by midafternoon we were hungry, despite our convictions, so we bought food through the fence from the outsiders.

But it wasn't enough to take a stand ourselves. The next day we saw many students returning to class, and I was enraged. I wanted *everyone* to join us. We had to stand in solidarity or the government would win. If the other girls didn't support the boycott voluntarily, I would make the decision for them.

At noon I followed a handful of girls into the meal room, and when I saw them carrying meal trays to their table, I came up behind them, pulled one girl's tray from her hands, and dumped it on the floor. Beans and boiled potatoes flew everywhere.

"You have to support the boycott," I cried. "If you don't stand with us, it will fail."

Pelin, behind me, stepped forward and yanked a tray from another girl, sending it onto the floor with the first. "Don't you care about your future?" she shouted.

Of course, this escalated matters. Our small world began to reflect the greater political upheaval going on all across our country. Just as the right wing was fighting the left wing in Turkey (which would result in a coup d'état a year later), our school was soon divided. Some of the girls just wanted to go quietly about their usual business, but we wouldn't let them. My group barred hallways and threatened to beat people up if they went to class. Personal choice was out the window. They would stand with us whether they wanted to or not. We wrote manifestos on large pieces of poster paper, pinned them on the walls, and educated people, telling them, "You are becoming slaves and will end up working for peanuts. The system is using you to their advantage." We saw nothing wrong with what we were doing. We were glorious followers of Karl Marx. At any moment, we believed, the government would capitulate and give us back our teaching certificates.

But, of course, it didn't happen that way. Eventually the police arrived. Questions were asked. The Ministry of Education issued the order that we were to settle down. We were determined not to. But our principal, a good and honorable man who was sincerely worried, pled with us.

"It's not going to go anywhere, and you're going to get arrested. This is not the way to achieve what you want."

In the end, we had to take the banner down. We went back to class. Nothing changed. Our first attempt to practice Communism had been a dismal failure. We graduated, heartbroken and angry, with three-year high-school diplomas, without teaching certificates, and with bad tastes in our mouths.

If it had remained a teacher's college, we wouldn't have had to take university entrance exams, but now we had to. I was particularly worried about this turn of events. Rich kids had tutors; I didn't. I could only go into the exams with what I knew on my own, and that was all. It was a good thing I had learned a lot in high school.

* * *

After the Great Boycott, I did a lot of thinking about my personal convictions and how I wanted to live my life. I had been raised in an atmosphere of conflicting beliefs. Dad believed in God, and the basic Muslim principles were always there, but he didn't follow Islam or accept the theology, per se. Mother lived in a totally different world, swinging like a pendulum, one day covering her head and then the next day putting on her make-up. Mustafa and Fatma were devout Muslims who wanted nothing to do with the outside or the political world. The schools I grew up in were full of principled, kind adults who taught me to value others but kept to a strictly secular line.

I wasn't sure where I personally stood. I saw good in various different philosophies, but I didn't feel I had found exactly the right way for me. Formal religion—as I knew it—held no attraction for me. Though my political convictions had received a sorry blow from our failed boycott, I remained idealistic and earnest. I sensed I had not yet found the perfect path for me.

* * *

The year was 1979, and the time came for the university placement examinations. It was a hot day in June. Having passed the first written entrance exam, I waited optimistically to go through the second one, the ability test. We prospective students were collected in a large room where several tables had been set up, one for each program. We were to go to the appropriate table and register, and then we were called one by one into an adjoining room for the tests.

I stood in the middle of that crowded room, looking at the lineups at each table, and felt my entire future hanging in the balance. Pelin had decided to be a chemical engineer and had been accepted into a program at the Middle East Technical University in Ankara. Much as I would have liked to stay with her, I knew that program wasn't for me. In my heart, I wanted to attend the Faculty of Law; I wanted to become a lawyer and change many things. I wanted to be a voice for the people who could not defend themselves in the legal system. But I knew that dream was never going to come true. As much as I yearned for the impossible at this time in my life, I knew the Faculty of Law wasn't going to be an option, largely because of the cost.

I thought the next best thing would be to become a physical education teacher. But when I located the table for that program, the lineup of students looked dauntingly long. It was stiflingly hot in the room, and I was getting hungry. I looked around some more and saw that the lineup for the music program was much shorter. Well, if I was confident enough to change directions, I was confident enough to sing. So I stepped into that line and registered for the placement exam in music instead. Thus was my fate determined by my impatience.

When it was my turn, I went into the adjoining room and faced a table with three teachers sitting behind it—two men and a woman. This was the jury that would judge each applicant.

"Name?" one of the teachers asked me, writing on a clipboard.

"Ayse Kizil."

"Where are you from?"

"Karaman, and before that, Istanbul."

"Age?"

The little voice in the back of my head whispered, *Pick a number, any number. Sixteen? Fourteen?* I stifled an inappropriate desire to giggle. "Nineteen," I said firmly.

"We will play some notes on the piano, and you will sing them. We are looking for accuracy in pitch," the teacher said. Standing, she went to an ancient piano at one side of the room. She played a series of notes slowly on the piano, like a bird pecking the keys, and I sang them back to her.

The teacher returned to the table and told me to choose any song I liked and sing it for them.

I had not prepared anything, of course, so I chose the first thing that came to mind—a children's Turkish folk song Dad had sometimes sung to me. I saw the teachers all writing furiously on their clipboards and wondered if the other students who were applying had sung more sophisticated songs, opera perhaps. Oh well, I had nothing to lose. I sang to the best of my ability and felt I'd done all right. My voice wasn't high—I was more of an alto—but it was strong and confident.

When I had finished, they asked a few basic questions about music theory, testing my knowledge of key signatures and time signatures. I was able to answer fairly well. And then they asked one last question. "What is it that first made you interested in music?"

I knew the answer immediately. "My father," I said promptly. "He would play opera and classical music on the radio at night, and we would listen to it together. It was . . . peaceful." I couldn't remember a time when music hadn't been part of my childhood, but it had become especially vital to me once we'd moved to Karaman. There had been such a comfort in sitting, he and I, listening to beautiful music together. It had made his mud-and-hay hut almost a make-believe world; there had been a surreal feel to it as the incongruous strains of Mozart and Stravinsky had floated out over the stark street. When I'd sat with my father, I'd been surrounded by safety and warmth, so different from the world outside that room. But I didn't know how to put all that I felt into words. All I could say was, "Music was the only bright glimmer of beauty in my life when I was growing up. It made my home bearable. It kept me company when I was at boarding school and when we left Istanbul. It was my friend."

There was a silence for a moment, and I wondered if I had said the wrong thing.

"Thank you, Miss Kizil," the teacher finally said, and her voice was quiet.

And that was it. I walked away, confident I would be accepted. I was never one to be easily intimidated, but I knew I had done well in this case. I was ready to reward myself with a meatball sandwich.

I met a classmate coming out of her examination, and we walked out into the street together.

"I hope I get in," she said, chewing on her lower lip. "I'm not sure I answered all the science questions correctly."

"If I get in, they gain a great person. If not, it's their loss," I declared. (As I said, humility was not my strength.) We laughed about it, wished each other luck, and parted ways.

Weeks later, the list of accepted applicants was posted on the university gate. I pushed through the crowd of students to look and saw my name on the list. I'd been accepted to the Faculty of Music. When I saw my name written there, I simply thought, "Oh well, I already knew that."

But now I had to tell the folks back home. That prospect I found more daunting than the examination. I returned to Karaman for the summer, where I slept on my bedroll in the communal bedroom and kept out of the house as much as I could. I told Dad, of course, what my plans were, and he was happy for me. But I swore him to secrecy.

"You're going to have to tell your parents eventually," he protested. "They'll have to know."

"I know. But the whole family is going to be upset by the news, especially Mustafa," I said. "I'll tell them but not until I have to, and then I'll do it in my own way. There's no point in upsetting everyone now and ruining my whole visit."

"All right, then, I will say nothing," Dad agreed.

So I kept my mouth shut around the others. I let them assume I was back in Karaman indefinitely. I did what I could to keep the peace, and when my temper or impatience got the better of me, I stayed away from the house. I eluded Mustafa's attempts to find me employment. The rest of the summer passed in relative quiet. Finally, it was the day before I was to leave for the university, and, of course, I couldn't put it off any longer.

That evening I put all my belongings in my suitcase and went into the other room, where everyone was gathering around the common pot for supper. They all looked up when I entered.

Taking a deep breath, I looked Mustafa in the eye and announced, "I have been accepted to Gazi University in Ankara. I am going to study music."

There was an electrified silence, and then everyone began talking at once. Fatma clapped her hands to her mouth. Mustafa stood up from his meal, snatched my suitcase out of my hand, and threw it at the wall, denting it and sending a shower of dirt to the floor. My heart jumped in my chest and started going double-time.

"What does a person need music for?" he cried. "What good will it do you? Can you earn a living with it?"

"Yes. I am going to study music," I repeated firmly, ignoring my fear. "I've already been accepted."

"Why do you insist on this? It is wrong for a woman to go so far from home."

"I want an education," I said.

"Why? What use is it to you?" he screamed. "Who is to pay for this?"

"My father will, and I will find work."

The mention of Dad fanned the flames. Mustafa's face was livid. "It is immoral. I forbid you to go. You will stay here where you belong."

I bit back the words I wanted to fling at him. *I have never belonged here.* There was no point in bringing that up and making things worse. This was my only chance to get away. I was determined to go to school, and that was that. He couldn't do anything to change it.

He could see the stubbornness in my face. Whirling round to face the back wall—beyond which was my father's room, where, no doubt, he was sitting alone at his meal and listening to all of this—Mustafa cried, "You are to blame for this. Giving her crazy ideas above her place in life. She leaves her family and her faith and goes to Ankara. She disobeys me, her *father*."

How dare he throw that in Dad's face, that he was my real father and not Dad? I felt a wave of fury wash over me, and it was all I could do not to fly at him with my fists. I drew myself up as tall as I could (I was in reality rather short, but I was still nearly as tall as Mustafa). The rest of the family was silent, staring at us both, waiting to see what would happen. Hatice cowered behind Fatma, clinging to her elbow.

"It isn't wrong for a woman to get an education," I declared. "I am going, and you can't stop me. I've been accepted. I take the bus tomorrow morning." I picked up my suitcase and faced him squarely, breathing hard.

He closed the gap between us. I could smell his breath when he thrust a finger in my face. "If you go," Mustafa hissed through gritted teeth, "never come back. You will not be welcome here."

"All right," I replied, and clutching my suitcase, I marched out of the house. I didn't look back or say good-bye to Cihangir. I marched around to the back of the house and went into Dad's room.

He was standing in the center of his tiny room, waiting for me. I dropped the suitcase, all dignity shredded, and ran into his arms. He let me wail for a while and then held me away from him by the shoulders to look down into my face.

"You are doing the right thing," he said. "You must go and learn all you can and find your own path. We both know your path is not here in Karaman."

"He was so angry," I said, wiping at my cheeks with my fingers. "He really meant what he said. I can never come back."

"Ayse," Dad said gently, "the day will come when Mustafa will be proud of your accomplishments. When you get your degree, your father will give you his own seat. You will see."

His words were softly spoken but had the aura of prophecy about them, and they calmed me. Taking a deep, shaky breath, I nodded.

"I believe you," I said.

"Sleep in here tonight, and tomorrow morning I will walk you to the bus."

In the end, it happened just the way Dad said. When I returned home years later with my degree, Mustafa stood and offered me his seat.

Section Three
Changes

Chapter Eleven

"I am with thee to save thee and to deliver thee."
—*Jeremiah 15:20*

I ATTENDED GAZI UNIVERSITY FROM 1979 until 1983. Ankara, the capital of Turkey, was built in a valley among softly rolling hills above the Sakarya River. It was known as Angora, until its name was changed in 1930, and that was where Angora goats, sheep, and rabbits came from. It was a modern commercial city of sizeable buildings, but not as cosmopolitan as Istanbul. There weren't really any skyscrapers, and most buildings were white stucco and stone. There were several big universities, hospitals, and an international airport. In spite of the surrounding hills, Ankara was in the driest part of Turkey, and it was very cold in winter and very hot in summer, with not many trees or much greenery. Aerial photos of the city showed it as quite desolate and monochromatic, but to me it was beautiful, because it was not Karaman.

I lived in a small, tenth-floor dorm room with five other girls. We each had a locker for our belongings, and there were three sets of bunk beds, a table, and six rickety chairs—that was basically all. It felt a lot like living at my high school. There was a metal fire escape on the outside of the building. The doors were locked at ten on weeknights and eleven on weekends, and after the cutoff time, no one was supposed to go in or out. But I needed desperately to work. I wasn't technically allowed to work as a student, but I was badly in need of money. So at night I sneaked out of the dormitory and down the fire escape and worked in Ankara, selling bus tickets at the bus depot. I sneaked back to the dorm in the morning. None of my roommates ever told on me; no doubt they were up to adventures of their own by means of that handy fire escape.

Ankara was the crossroads of both the country's rail and highway systems. The bus depot was crowded and smelly. At certain times of the night, vendors sold food in the station—meat and onions in pita bread—and then the station smelled good. But when the food wasn't being sold, the smell in the station was not nice.

I was the only female working at the bus station and was a great favorite among the others. I was able to travel all over Turkey by bus for free, so I saw many cities throughout Turkey at a whirlwind pace, crammed into weekends, when I didn't have school. I traveled through the Marmara region, where Europe meets Asia beside the Black Sea, with its golden sunflower fields and olive groves. I saw the rich blue waters of the Aegean coast and the famous ruins of Troy, that city made legendary in Homer's *Iliad*. I saw stark mountain ranges and the wide River Firat, went clear to the Iranian border, and saw the big dam in Elazig. When I visited the dam, it was February, and the water was freezing, but I waded out into it up to my waist. (I admit I had been drinking at the time and don't really remember the cold.) It was a foolish thing to do, but I wanted to experience every sensation and live life deeply. I grew to appreciate Turkey's rich treasures of history and scenery. There was so much about my land I didn't yet know, and I wanted to learn it all.

Because I couldn't miss classes, I often only had time to walk around for a few hours at my destination before heading straight back. Of course, I wasn't able to see much, mostly just what went past my bus window. But that wasn't the point of my travels. I went simply because I *could*. I relished the freedom, the novelty, the feeling of moving forward. I marveled at the sheer age of the things I saw that made my own short life seem like just a speck in the stretching eons of history. I drank in the new sights and smells, the colors of Turkey, and dreamt about traveling even farther one day.

University proved to be socially challenging. I was a loner, and not many people paid attention to anyone else. In high school, there had been sisterhood and comradery, but in university it was every man for himself. Through all the new experiences that came to me at the university, Dad remained the constant rock I relied on. We wrote to each other often, and his chatty letters were nearly as good as conversations in person. Once when I was sick, he sent a telegram asking if I was okay because he hadn't heard from me. This told me he relished our written conversations as much as I did. The only thing he did not tell me in those newsy letters was that he was ill. For a long time, he didn't know it himself, but when he learned about his cancer, he kept the truth from me.

I soon discovered that music suited me. Though I had fallen into it without any planning, it turned out to be the right program for me. Dad had always encouraged me to learn languages and play instruments. I wanted to play violin, but my teachers said my hand structure wasn't right for violin, so I was assigned to piano. This I diligently pursued, but to this day, I still prefer the soothing honey sounds of the violin and cello.

I got very good grades. I loved music, and I loved my new life. Now, years later and half a world away, I constantly listen to music and have stereos in almost every room of my house. In times of sadness, I rely on music to pull me through.

Back in that mud room in Karaman, as I had listened to music with my father, he had told me about going to dressy concerts at music halls in Istanbul when he was younger, about the great singers he had heard. I never saw a concert until I was at the university. Music allowed me to bring Dad with me, in a sense, when I was in Ankara, and it brings him close to me now. Whenever I hear classical music or opera, I remember my childhood and my wonderful father sitting by his radio in his barren room. It makes me think of what has been lost over the years and what has been added. When I hear opera, I am in a safe place.

* * *

Throughout high school and increasingly in university, I struggled with occasional bouts of deep depression. Even though intellectually I understood this to be a reasonable reaction to the abuse, loss, and change I had experienced in my short life, I still had to deal with it emotionally. Sometimes I could keep the depression at bay by working myself to exhaustion or throwing myself into my activities with ferocious energy—I may be little, but there is a lot of stamina in my small frame—but sometimes the depression got the upper hand, and the energy would drain from me so that I found it difficult to do anything or take an interest in anything. At those times, life became very dark in severe contrast to my usually optimistic disposition. On seven occasions, I attempted suicide by overdose and other methods, but I always left a note for others to find so I could be rescued. I knew just what to do so my stomach could be pumped in time to save me.

Years later when I discussed this dark period of time with a psychiatrist, he told me, "You weren't ready to die. You didn't intend to die."

"It felt like I did at the time," I said dryly. "All seven times, in fact."

"No," he insisted. "There are many ways to die instantly, and you didn't choose any of them. You always went with a method from which you could be rescued, and you made sure the circumstances were such that you would be saved in time. There are two reasons you didn't really kill yourself. One was the intense attention you received. It made you feel important and cared for. You wanted the world to notice you were there."

"Maybe so," I conceded reluctantly. The doctors and nurses certainly had noticed me and paid attention. But it was too much like Turkan's constant bid for attention, and I didn't want to accept it. "And the second reason?"

"You were slowly trying to erase yourself off the planet," he said with a wink, "but your eraser wasn't big enough."

* * *

In 1981, I had a strange and disturbing experience that is difficult to describe. I was on a bus trip by myself, traveling for free, as always, and it was as if I lost consciousness. I can't describe it in any other way. I must have had a sort of mental breakdown or gone into a fugue state, and I only know what happened from what witnesses later told me. I apparently got off the bus in a distant southern city with the intention of visiting some friends in their home. It was a ten-hour ride from Ankara. For some reason, I completely lost my memory. My friends met me at the station and took me to their home for three days, but I talked incoherently, and they didn't know what to make of it. Not sure what to do and not wanting to get involved in this strange situation, my friends' parents put a name tag on my clothing and sent me by bus to the nearest big city, Adana. Perhaps they were hoping some kind person would take me to the city hospital, where I could get medical care. I wandered the bus station in Adana, where friendly strangers gave me tea, but they didn't know what else to do for me, so in the end, someone else pinned another note to my chest and sent me to the hospital.

I was in the hospital for seven days, and the doctors couldn't figure out what was wrong with me. My vital signs were failing. My brain was shutting down, and I slipped into a coma. There was no response when the doctors poked me with needles. Finally, no vital signs were detectable at all, and I was declared dead and taken to the hospital morgue. I have no recollection of this at all. Fortunately, a short time later, a cleaner saw me move and alerted the doctors. I was whisked back up to the hospital ward and revived, but doctors still couldn't diagnose my problem. They decided my ailment must not be physical, and they admitted me to the mental health unit, where I stayed for twenty-one days. I still had no memory, and no one knew who I was.

If one can describe "hell on earth," this place would fit that description perfectly. The unit was crowded with patients, and someone was always crying or lamenting about something. Their pain became my pain, but I was no use to anyone, including myself. I didn't know who I was or why I was there. All I knew was I had no energy left in my body. I couldn't even sit up in my bed but could only lie helplessly. I felt a great sense of loss and sadness. I was completely alone, and I felt that not even God Himself could help me here. All I could do was cry. I wanted to cry forever. Perhaps this was the ultimate depths of depression. Perhaps it was my way of cleansing my burdened soul and repenting of my mistakes.

In high school, I'd had a problem with stealing, perhaps because I'd had so much taken from me so abruptly throughout my life. Whatever the reason, I had once stolen a little white ceramic angel from a store and had given it to Dad as a present. Not knowing where it had come from, he valued it and said it reminded him of me. The same date that I went into a coma, my dad, miles and miles away, accidentally knocked the angel over, and it fell and broke into three pieces. He said he knew at that moment that something was wrong with me, and he began to make inquiries. He contacted people. He found out I was missing from school and that the university was also looking for me. No one had any idea where I'd gone.

Meanwhile, in the mental institution, I was vaguely aware of the other patients. I remember there was a woman who'd lost a child and would clasp a stone and rock it back and forth like a baby. She would sing lullabies to it in a hushed voice to comfort her imaginary child. When I watched her, I felt great sorrow because she was hugging that stone with the great care and love I wished my mother would have had for me. Though my memory was locked away somewhere in the back of my mind, temporarily inaccessible, I somehow felt that lack of motherly love acutely. But I couldn't communicate it to anyone.

There was an insomniac woman in the ward, and I became an insomniac just watching her. Day after day, night after night, I watched her in silence. She never spoke. She lay on her bed and stared at my face, and I stared at hers.

The hospital walls were white and bare. I hated being in that hospital bed but was also grateful at the same time that I had a warm place to stay. Nothing seemed important to me, and I lost all sense of time. I just lay in my bed day after day, crying. Days and nights took on the same aspect. Even the hot sunlight coming through the window didn't warm my heart. I was so severely depressed that life and death were only separated by an invisible, thin line. There were days I honestly didn't know if I was dead or alive, and come to think of it, I didn't particularly care which I was. I felt as if I were grieving for all the things I had never had, all the things that had been taken from me, and all the things I was never going to have. It was too much loss for one person to bear.

I couldn't eat or sleep, and I lost weight, going down to about eighty-five pounds. (I was already petite to begin with.) Time passed, and then one day I became aware of the tangy smell of oranges coming in through the open window. I realized I wanted to eat oranges. Little by little, I started waking up, returning slowly to life.

There was a nurse at the nurses' station who used to listen to music programs on a little, portable, battery-operated radio. I heard the music and sang along, and I found that I knew many of the songs, though I didn't know how I knew them. The nurse noticed me singing and let me listen to the radio with her. She talked to me and realized there must be something about me to do with music. Bit by bit, my memory was returning, but I still had trouble communicating with anyone. The nurse was curious and sympathetic, and she wanted to help me find out who I was and where I'd come from. Based on the age she guessed me to be, she deduced I must be a student. She contacted different music faculties—there weren't many—and eventually found the university I had attended and learned that they were looking for me. The hospital bought me a ticket home to Karaman, stuck a name tag on my chest once again, and put me back on the bus with a plastic bag containing my clothes. All the clothing I had with me, I had stolen from other people back home.

When I arrived back in Karaman, it was late at night, and I felt very sick. However, I knew that nothing I carried in my bag was really mine, and I was determined to give back every item I had stolen from each house to show my gratitude that I was recovering and finally in a familiar place. Before I even went home, I first walked around Karaman for a long time, delivering the stolen items to the doorsteps of the rightful owners. That dark night was a turning point in my life. There, in the middle of nowhere, I made a promise never to steal anything again from anyone as long as I lived, and I have kept that promise.

After this sad but sobering journey, I made my way home to Dad's little room and slept for four solid days. I was malnourished and weak and was seeing double. My father cared for me, immensely relieved that I had been found. My memory returned over time, but I never remembered the events of the past month myself; I only base this account on what others have told me. I have never fully understood what happened to me and have never received a proper diagnosis. Many years later I went to a specialist to figure out what had occurred. I asked my doctor about possibly undergoing hypnosis to try to retrieve my memory of what had happened during that episode when I'd lost myself. He wisely told me, "Nothing good will come of it. Just leave it alone." He advised me to forget about it and get on with my life. He indicated that the human brain is very protective, and when it can't endure more pain, it shuts itself down. Whatever it was protecting me from would probably not be something good to remember anyway. So I have left it alone.

My health gradually improved, and my strength returned. I went back to Ankara, and the university kindly allowed me to take the final exams despite my lengthy absence. I passed, so my year was not wasted. That period of my life remains largely a mystery to me, but I have decided not to dwell on it too much. I take from it a lesson in grace and the kindness of strangers and move on.

* * *

My life at school resumed, but during the next semester, I could tell from my father's letters that he wasn't feeling well. He never explicitly said it, but I could read between the lines that he wasn't his usual energetic, positive self. When he didn't come to see me for some time, I became concerned about him, so I went to see him on one of my rare visits to Karaman. I thought perhaps he was just tired. But when I arrived, I found him lying on his bed in his little room, which was unusual for him in the daytime. He looked pale and had lost a lot of weight. He had always been tall and thin, but the weight loss was noticeable now.

When he saw me, he smiled and wanted to get up. I told him to stay where he was and pulled up a chair to sit beside him.

"Dad, how are you doing?" I asked.

"Oh, well, I'm fine." He tried to shrug it off, but I wouldn't accept his answer.

"Dad, I really want to know the truth. Tell me."

He looked at me silently for a moment, and I was alarmed to see tears welling in his eyes.

"I went to the doctor, Ayse," he said at last.

This shocked me because he had never gone to the doctor in his life—ever, not even for a checkup. I knew something was terribly wrong.

I took his hand and held it in mine. I looked him in the eye and said, "Now are you going to tell me what's wrong?"

The tears spilled over, which I had only seen happen once before, on that dreadful day he had left me at school. It made me cry too.

"I have cancer," he said simply. "It is so advanced that there is no coming back from it. I am going to die. I don't know when."

I was shattered. The reality of it was hard to grasp. I struggled to keep my voice calm. "Is there anything I can do for you, Dad?" I asked.

Dad squeezed my hand with his. "You just continue to be my daughter and live your life as if I'm always there," he said gently.

I nodded, unable to speak for a moment, and then asked him, "Have you told Mom?"

Dad's eyes flashed an intense blue, and he declared firmly, "She never was interested in my health. I'm not going to tell her."

"All right. Don't upset yourself."

"I have also decided I'm going to divorce her."

I couldn't see the point of that at this stage, and I could see several reasons against it. "Dad, you've hung on this long. Don't do that. She isn't a well person, and if you do it, she'll be out on the street with her mental illness. If you divorce her, she won't get your pension. And if she doesn't get your pension, who will look after her? Nobody."

He thought for a moment and then told me he saw my point. "All right. But that doesn't mean I want to see her or talk to her. I don't even want her to come to my funeral."

We spoke quietly together for a long time, and then he told me he felt a little better and sat up in his bed. I sat next to him on the bed and hugged him. We sat together in silence for a while, just enjoying each other's company in that tiny mud room where we'd spent so much time together. I told myself that one day he wasn't going to be there anymore. I tried to imagine it and couldn't. I didn't even want to think about it. It was very hard to leave him and go back to school.

Several months later, in September 1982, I was in Istanbul visiting a friend, and I had a dream that my dad came to me dressed all in white. He told me he had deposited his last check and there would be no more money forthcoming. I didn't understand the dream, but the next day a telegram came telling me he had died. I could only press that slip of paper to my chest and rock back and forth, overwhelmed with grief and disbelief. My father, my friend, was gone. It was the saddest moment of my life; nothing has ever equaled it.

I took the bus straight home to Karaman. It dropped me at the side of the road in the same place Dad, Cihangir, and I had landed eight years earlier with only the clothes on our backs. The smell of manure bombarded me the same way it had that first day. I didn't take time to go through the gate but jumped the low stone wall and headed for Mustafa and Fatma's house. A neighbor saw me and gave a shout. I turned impatiently to face him.

"You are too late," he called to me.

"What?"

"They buried Necmi Gencata four days ago."

I stood, too stunned to move. They must have delayed sending the telegram. I was too late. He was buried, and I would never see his beautiful face again.

I didn't stop to think. I turned right around, jumped back over the wall, and went back to Ankara on the same bus I'd just arrived on. I did not see Cihangir or the others. I simply fled. I felt I was traveling in a fog. Nothing seemed real.

When the bus reached a stopover, I got off and stretched my legs with the other passengers. I wandered down the road a distance, away from the others, where no one could see my tears. That stopover was the one and only time I let myself cry over my father. At the passage of the Bolu Mountain, I yelled my great pain at the rocks, with the fog all around me and the cold air filling my lungs. Was the grave this cold for my father too? Such loneliness enveloped me as I realized I could never have another conversation with him. I had never known such desolation.

A few minutes later, I pulled myself together and spoke aloud to the fog. I made a promise to my dad that from that day on, I would become the daughter he deserved to have rather than what I was then becoming. And then I got back on the bus.

Chapter Twelve

"Thou feedest them with the bread of tears; and givest them tears to drink in great measure."
—Psalm 80:5

WITHOUT DAD'S SUPPORT, MY FINANCIAL situation became desperate. I missed the deadline for residence in the government-owned dormitory and couldn't get in. Out of desperation, I agreed to live with an elderly woman who gave me a room in exchange for taking care of her. It was far from the university, but it was my only solution. The room did not include meals, and I received no pay for caring for her. To save money, I walked to and from school, two and a half hours each way every day. My feet would grow hot through the bottoms of my shoes from the sun-baked road, and by the time I arrived home in the evening, it would be nearly dark. I would watch cars and buses go past me and wish someone I knew would come along and give me a ride, but it never happened. I walked with my chin up and my stride strong, showing the world I wasn't defeated.

But even without having to pay for my room, it was difficult to make ends meet. I began saving money by eating only every other day. It was a trial to care for this woman and live in her home and smell the meals she made for herself but not be able to take part in them. I was too proud to beg food from her, and she never offered. Sometimes I ate out of garbage cans, making sure no one was looking before I did it. The first time I did that, it was as if a line had been crossed; some part of me had given in. I refused to think less of myself for it though. I told myself I had to survive; I would do whatever it took. If no one else looked kindly on me, at least I would look kindly on myself. But it seemed I never had enough energy, and my gums began to soften and bleed. I lost two of my teeth from malnutrition, and I lost my toenails.

In spite of the difficulties, I was determined to finish school. I was thirsty for education. In a big city, it was normal for women to be educated, but in Karaman, it was not the norm. No one else in my biological family had made it past high school, and even now many of the younger generation still drop out before graduating. The child of a well-off or established family could expect to go to school, but from a challenged family, no. In that society, education for women was considered a great luxury, not a necessity. But to me it *was* a necessity. And I knew Dad would have wanted me to finish.

Finally, things were so desperate financially that I swallowed my pride and wrote to ask Turkan for money. She was living in Karaman by then. I didn't hold out a lot of hope, but it was worth a try. Two days later she sent a telegram saying, "No, you should find a rich husband and marry him. You're not my problem." I still have the telegram.

But I would not let go of my dreams or the future I had planned for myself. Somehow, though, as I planned that future, marriage and family were not really part of it. I had never liked wedding gowns and never thought I would wear one. No one would ever choose to marry me. I didn't consider myself a good catch. But one day, the elderly woman I was caring for and I watched Lady Diana's wedding on TV. I saw the princess's beautiful dress, like a creamy meringue flowing around her, saw her radiant face, and I thought, *Why not me?*

There is a Turkish saying: The easiest money you can spend is somebody else's. The easiest pain you can endure is somebody else's.

* * *

Some time after Dad died, Turkan left Karaman as suddenly as she had arrived. A little while later, I received word through neighbors that she had gone to Cukurbag, where she was living like a pauper. I knew she had Dad's pension to live on, as they had never divorced, so money wasn't a problem. Not sure what to make of this, I went one weekend to visit her.

Cukurbag being such a small place, I had only to inquire of the first villager I met, and he was able to point me in the right direction. To my astonishment, he led me not to a house but to a cave in the rocks at the edge of the village, a cave meant for a stable. I climbed up the dusty path and found Turkan sitting quietly on a wooden chair just inside the entrance to the cave. She looked like any dignified woman sitting at the door of her home waiting for visitors . . . except there was no door and no home.

"Good afternoon," I said formally because her position, her expression, and her erect posture seemed to require formality.

"Hello, Ayse," she said warmly. I was glad she at least recognized me; there were times she hadn't.

"How are you?"

"Well, thank you. And you?"

I felt as if we were doing one of my English grammar exercises at school. I decided to get right to the subject. "I understand you are living here now, Mother," I said carefully, not letting my voice sound judgmental.

She nodded. "Yes, and the rent is quite low."

I peered past her into the cave and saw the rough-hewn walls, the stone floor, albeit it had been swept clean. There was a bed tucked to one side, and a small table with one more chair filled another side. Against the wall, I saw a couple of cardboard boxes, which must have held her clothes and things. That was all. I was appalled that she was actually paying rent to stay in this awful, primitive place.

"May I come in and sit down?" I asked her.

"She never lets anyone in," the villager said behind me. "She won't talk to anyone."

"Of course my daughter can come in," Mother objected.

I went into the cave and looked around and found there really was no more to it than I had seen at first glance.

"There's no stove," I pointed out. "How will you keep it warm in the winter? You know how cold it gets."

Mother turned her head away and looked out over the hillside without speaking, and I mentally kicked myself for the comment. Of course she wouldn't have a stove; Mother was extremely afraid of burning to death. Hadn't I spent my childhood listening to her express her terror of dying by fire?

"But how will you heat your . . . house?" I asked again.

"Angels will heat my house," she replied with finality.

Whenever I visited her after that, I would ask the question. "Mother, how do you survive all the cold winter months in this place?" and she would always just smile and answer, "Angels heat my house."

I really do wonder how she survived the cold in that cave. Maybe she was right.

Mother had no plumbing, so she used a bucket, which she would carry and empty out in the fields at the edge of town. She would wash her hands with her bar of soap at the common fountain at the entrance of the village, just as she had for hours at the sink back in our apartment in Istanbul. Because she used so much soap, there would be nothing but soapy water everywhere. The shepherds would bring their goats and sheep home from grazing, and the animals would stop to drink that soapy water at the fountain. This continued day after day, and, of course, it caused the animals severe bowel problems. The villagers became upset because the animals left the roads in horrible condition as a result. The villagers got together and came to Mother's door and demanded that she not wash her hands at the fountain anymore.

Every year, I went especially to visit her. She wouldn't let me stay there, so it was a short visit, but I went. I'm not sure why I felt I needed to do this. My feelings toward her were ambivalent; I wasn't sure that I loved her or hated her. I think I probably feared her a little. I didn't feel an obligation to make sure she was all right—she certainly had more money than I did, even if she chose not to spend it on housing. But somehow I felt it was something I needed to do—whether for her or for me or for Dad, I didn't know; nor did I think about it very much. She had raised me, in whatever broken way she could manage, and now I kept track of her.

* * *

The early 1980s were known as the terrorist years in my country, a time of civil disorder and Islamic extremism. The military took administrative control of the state, and martial law was set in place in every province of Turkey. Activists fought each other with words, fists, and weapons. The discord was hottest among the students and young adults. It was a natural age for separating from the "establishment" and challenging authority, an age at which it is both common and expected that a person will explore his or her own identity and form a personal philosophy by which to conduct life. But we carried it to an extreme. We students were all about change, and we wanted to make a difference in the world, but we had tunnel vision when it came to actually going about it. Unfortunately, passions run high in young adulthood, and idealism doesn't always leave room for tolerance or patience. Often this found expression in demonstrations of overt violence. Thousands of right-wing students marched down one street, and thousands of left-wing students marched down another street, and we met in front of the university. Most often it ended up in a fight, and the police were always there, trying to disperse the crowd with water or beatings.

As an idealist and committed Marxist who hadn't learned much from the Great Boycott, I was also involved. I managed to stay one step ahead of the police, but I saw many of my friends arrested. They went into the police station and never came out again, and their deaths were officially ruled as suicides, though we all knew the chilling truth. Rather than frightening us off, this only increased the intensity of our convictions. I smothered my fear and insecurity with anger, riding it to heady heights that made me feel invincible.

When situations grew too dangerous, we would run away to "safe spots" where we knew other leftists gathered, much as gangs today have "territories" that belong to them. One of these safe spots was the Middle East Technical University, where Pelin was studying. I was essentially homeless at that time, having left the elderly woman I'd been caring for, and I would go there to sleep on the floor in the dorms with fellow activists, seeking safety in numbers. I have always been interested in people and trying to understand what motivates them—the forces that influence a group of ordinarily polite and well-behaved young people to resort to behavior that, in other political circumstances, they would not think to be involved in. I suppose in my case, I was looking for more than just an outlet for my beliefs and vision. It went beyond making a political statement. I was looking for a group to which I could belong, a family in a sense, seeking out the company of others who seemed as lost and angry and ungrounded as I was. Whatever the case, we leftists hung out together, and that was where I met Tim.

Tim was a Nigerian student living in the dorms. He was tall, full of energy, and passionate in his convictions. He had a clear vision of where he wanted to go in life and had political aspirations. I, whose future was foggy, gravitated to him and his confident circle. He had four friends, other men from Nigeria, who lived in a house near the university. When they heard I was homeless, they kindly offered me a place in their house. (Marxists believe in brotherhood, after all.)

At first I hesitated to accept their generous offer. Even though I was not a practicing Muslim, I still knew it was overstepping bounds for a single female to move in with four single men. While the Marxist brotherhood might understand it, society at large may not look so kindly on it. But in the end, I knew I couldn't keep up a life of moving from place to place. I decided it would be safer and cheaper for me to stay with them. They were courteous and protective and became like brothers to me. I never had to fear any of them crossing boundaries.

Tim and I spent a lot of time talking about his vision of the future and the political goals he held. He took me to meetings and rallies, explaining to me a lot about how government systems worked, and I came to share his philosophy. It seemed like the next logical step to share a common path in life too, so after a while, Tim and I became engaged. Looking back on it, I think I sort of fell into it without a lot of thought. Our plans were rather vague, with no set time line, because our lives were filled with turmoil. To be honest, I suppose part of the reason I was drawn to him was my own rebellious streak; I was defiant of cultural norms. I saw Marxism as being all about going against "the system." Marrying a non-Muslim Nigerian was about as countercultural as it got.

I was so bold as to take Tim home to Karaman with me once. My family had no idea what to make of it or how to treat him. Even Mustafa was startled into uncharacteristic silence. The children in our neighborhood had never seen a black person before, and they followed him around the streets as we walked, wanting to touch his chocolate skin. Tim took all the awkward attention in stride, unperturbed, and I told myself that here was a man I could trust to handle any situation that might arise. I tried to think what Dad would have thought of him, but I wasn't sure. I like to think he would have admired Tim's keen mind and reformist outlook. He certainly would have approved of Tim's energy and confidence.

Tim's mother visited once. She was polite but cool and never did seem to warm up to me. After she returned home, she sent a letter to Tim asking him to leave me. After receiving the letter, Tim came to see me one afternoon, and we went for a walk.

"I'm afraid my mother didn't like you," he said bluntly.

"Why not?" I was dismayed. Even though we had no plans to live with or near her, I knew it was best if one could get along with one's mother-in-law. I didn't want Tim to be torn, having to mediate between us. I had been as courteous to her as I could be, and I didn't think I had made any faux pas.

Then he slid his dark eyes away from me in embarrassment, and I understood.

"It's because I'm white, isn't it?" I said.

He spread his large hands. "You have to understand. I am planning to return to Nigeria and go into politics. My mother thinks having a white wife will be a stumbling block for me."

"Is that true? Would I hinder your career?"

"I don't know," he admitted. "But I'm not letting that stop me."

I let his words reassure me and told myself I should be optimistic and everything would work out for the best. A new constitution had been accepted in Turkey in 1982, and although military rule didn't end until late the following year, it seemed to me to be a sign of hope that our cause would win out in the end. Anything that spoke of hope, I clung to.

* * *

It was around this time that I consciously chose to leave Islam. I had never been observant, and I didn't like the thought of rules confining me. I felt formal religion imposed someone else's vision on my freedom, and I had a hard time believing in any god that would allow such turmoil and bitterness in the world. As a child, I had enjoyed celebrating Ramazan Bayrami and Kurban Bayrami, Islamic holidays of great significance. Turkan had always gone out of her way to make those holidays special for us, giving us candy, money, and gifts. In high school, I had usually spent the holidays in others' homes and hadn't returned to Karaman often. But in university, I saw no point in celebrating them anymore; I didn't believe in their religious foundation, and I felt restless and discouraged at holiday times. I hated the fact that during the holidays everybody else was happy and I wasn't.

I believed only in man's ability to direct his own fate and form society as he saw fit. Along with being a Communist, I basically became an atheist.

I promised myself I would never live someone else's dream—only my own. Still nursing old wounds, I also vowed my tears would be only for myself and my father and no one else. Crying never helps. So I grew tough and determined, refusing self-pity. I became rather fierce. I also became an alcoholic.

Islam forbids the use of alcohol or tobacco. However, I no longer had faith in those beliefs, if indeed I ever had, and I found myself turning more and more to these substances. Alcohol grew to be a disturbing companion in my miserable existence. I have never liked having to rely on anyone or anything, but I found myself becoming increasingly reliant on alcohol as a means of coping with the difficulties in my life. I wrongly saw it as my friend, thinking that it was helping me numb myself and escape emotions I didn't want. I hid in alcohol to help me ignore the problems I couldn't seem to solve. I gained new insight into Omer and what drove him to find solace in drinking. However, addictions and vices cost money, and I had none. I worked odd jobs here and there as I could find them, but money was always very tight. I would follow people on the street and collect the cigarette butts they dropped so I could smoke them. I smoked the equivalent of two packs a day. But I never did drugs.

But toughness and apathy are difficult burdens to carry. Eventually I realized this was not the way to live. I had seen cancer kill my beloved dad and knew smoking could increase my own chances of having a similar fate. I knew I had to quit both smoking and drinking. The alcohol was not my friend; it was my enemy, taking away my freedom of choice. Guilt filled me when I admitted I was not being the daughter Dad deserved to have. After a very dismal and depressing few years, I gathered together my courage and quit one day, "cold turkey"—a funny phrase but appropriate. I determined to rely on myself alone; I had yet to learn to rely on God.

Tim's situation, meanwhile, had become complicated. There was political turmoil in Nigeria and because of the uprising, he was unable to get money from home, which caused him difficulty affording the basic necessities.

"I will help you," I told him when we were discussing it one day, completely ignoring the fact that I could barely afford the necessities myself. This was my future husband; of course I would give him all I had.

"How can you? You have less money than I do," he pointed out.

"I'll find work," I promised. "I can make more money working abroad than I can in Turkey. As soon as I can arrange it, I'll go."

Without any more thought than that, I committed myself to the idea. I began the paperwork to become a nanny in Saudi Arabia. Once again my life seemed to be shifting abruptly in a new direction, unplanned and unprepared for.

* * *

Sometimes life changes because we take action; sometimes it changes because we *don't* take action. And sometimes it changes because God has different plans in mind for us than we have planned for ourselves. Even while I called myself an atheist, I could sense the hand of a higher power directing me toward the way I should go. Now, of course, many years later, I can recognize that influence for what it was: the Spirit working to bring me to the path I needed to take.

In the winter of 1984, my arrangements for Saudi Arabia had not yet gone through, and I was working in an Ankara real estate agency as a secretary while I waited. It provided a small but steady income and improved my life a great deal. I was alone in the office one day, vacuuming and tidying up, when the bell on the door rang and I turned to see a man enter. He nodded at me and took a seat in one of the chairs in the reception area. I figured he was waiting for one of the agents, and I continued vacuuming.

As I worked my way closer, I got a better look at him. I thought him very fair and handsome, with his pale skin and light brown hair. His clothes were neat and clean, and he was clean-shaven. Definitely not Turkish. Perhaps American. I drew closer with my vacuum, and he looked up at me. I was taken aback by the blueness of his eyes. They were the most beautiful eyes, not just in their color but in their expression. He looked kind.

"Move your feet," I said, showing off my English. To this day, I can't believe those were the first words I ever said to him.

He moved his feet. I continued to clean around him. Occasionally I would sneak a look at him, and every time I looked, I caught him sneaking a look at me. There was something indefinable about him that kept drawing my attention. I was suddenly very conscious of my every move, my hair, my hands. I wasn't sure how to arrange my face. I peeked at him again and once more caught him watching me, and we both smiled.

I finished my work and put away the vacuum. Now I had a dilemma. I had to close the office for lunch, and somehow I had to let this man know the agents were away and would not be back until after lunch. But I didn't know enough English to convey all this.

I tried speaking to him in Turkish, but he only smiled again, spread his hands, and shook his head. He didn't know a word of the language. But I liked his lovely smile.

"I eat," I said in English, dredging up everything I could remember from my school days. "You go now. Come back." I pantomimed closing and locking the door and then tapped my watch. "One hour. My boss, one hour."

The man stood—he was quite a bit taller than I—and nodded, showing he understood. But at the door, he paused, and I wondered if I had not managed to communicate after all. The man looked back at me and said carefully, "You eat with me?" He was asking me to lunch.

I was surprised. A foreigner approaching a Turkish girl just wasn't done. But aside from that, how could someone like him show interest in someone like me? I was caught off guard by the strong feeling of delight that came over me. Without hesitation, I grinned, stepped forward, and said yes.

He held out a hand to shake mine (another North American clue), and his grasp was strong and warm. "My name is Ross Hitchins," he said.

"Ayse," I said. "Ayse Kizil."

We went to lunch, and in a very broken and hindered way, we talked. My English vocabulary consisted of eight hundred to a thousand words, and those were mostly nouns and a few verbs. We used a lot of pantomime and sometimes were reduced to drawing stick figures on paper napkins, but we managed to communicate. I learned Ross was Canadian and worked for de Havilland (now known as Bombardier). He had been sent as a technical advisor to Turkish Airlines, assigned first to Istanbul and then to Ankara, where the airport was. He was staying in a hotel, but he wanted to rent a place of his own instead since he was going to be in Turkey for some time. That was why he had come to the real estate agency. I sensed he was a patient and kind man with a sense of humor, and I enjoyed our crazy conversation.

After eating, we went back to the office, and he spoke to an agent. I returned to my desk and tried not to look like I was eavesdropping. The agent spoke much better English than I did, and I was envious of his ability to speak freely with Ross. When Ross's conversation with the agent was completed, he came back into the lobby, smiled at me, shook my hand again, then told me good-bye and left. I watched him walk away down the street. When I returned home that night, I kept thinking about this polite, friendly man from Canada. I wondered if I would see him again and if we would talk again. I sincerely hoped so.

Chapter Thirteen

"Therefore shall ye lay up these my words
in your heart and in your soul."
—*Deuteronomy 11:18*

Ross came back to the agency the very next day. This time he was armed with a Turkish tourist's phrase book. It was not very helpful unless he wanted to ask me the way to the bus station or direct a waiter to bring the bill, but I found a secondhand English-Turkish dictionary that was more useful. We passed it back and forth between us, slowly and painfully deciphering what the other said. In ordinary conversations, I generally found that people tended to miss much of what was said because of inattention or because they were thinking of what they were going to say next when the other person stopped speaking. But because communication was so difficult for Ross and me, we each really had to focus on what the other was trying to say, hanging on every word and really concentrating. This made for a much more intense and intimate interaction. It was more like attempting to read each other's minds than carrying on a verbal dialogue. In this way, we began to learn about each other.

We met a few times after that for informal discussions. Mostly we chatted about his life and my life, doing a cultural comparative analysis. He told me about Canada and the weather there, his mother, his employment. We compared our respective government systems and political climates. I told him about school, my interest in music, and Istanbul, and we compared it to Toronto. But I didn't tell him much about Karaman or my family or the mixed-up childhood I'd had. As we delved into each other's minds, my first impression of him only intensified; I had never met anyone like him before, and I enjoyed his company very much. When we spent time together, I could never seem to get my fill of just looking at him. His voice warmed me, whether or not I understood his words.

One day, Ross asked formally, "Will you go out with me?"

"Yes," I said.

He looked relieved. "Great, then we can go—"

"No."

He stopped, eyebrows raised. "Do you want to go out with me?"

"Yes."

"Then we can go—"

"No." In my "Tarzan English," I tried to explain that I would like to go on a date, but most Turkish girls didn't date. It just wasn't done. In his "Tarzan Turkish," Ross tried to argue his position. And then for the first time, I told him I was engaged to Tim, an African idealist and soon-to-be politician. To my surprise, this didn't seem to discourage Ross. He told me he also had a girlfriend, Bonnie, back in Canada . . . and this didn't discourage me either. So we agreed to go out. And then he continued to ask me to dinner or out for walks or to go to the market with him, ostensibly to help translate, though we both knew this was not the real reason. We just wanted to spend time together.

One day after one of our talks, Ross decided I was the girl for him—though he didn't tell me so at the time. Much later, he shared with me that on that day he realized he and his girlfriend back in Canada were not meant for each other. He felt he and I were drawn to each other in a way he and Bonnie had never been. But he experienced an inner battle with himself because he was Mormon and I was Muslim, and he didn't know how to reconcile that vital difference. But he said he had recognized from the first time he'd seen me that I was something special.

It was very clear to me from the outset that Ross was different from anyone else I knew. It was not just his nationality or career that set him apart. He didn't smoke or drink. He didn't use bad language. He valued my opinions and was kind and gentle, and I felt he treated me as a real, valid, beautiful person. Compared to the group I ran around with, Ross was soft-spoken and peaceful. He didn't believe in violent means to obtain a goal, nor did he have great political dreams of turning the world upside down. And yet he was rapidly doing just that to my personal world.

I asked him a lot of questions about why he was different, and Ross told me he was LDS and that he wanted to date and marry only an LDS woman. I didn't know what *LDS* was. With the dictionary getting a good workout between us, he began to tell me about his religion, The Church of Jesus Christ of Latter-day Saints. He explained its unusual beginnings and history, the way it had grown, and the basic principles the Church taught and stood for. He told me about living prophets, eternal marriage, and families being sealed for eternity instead of being together just until death.

Everything Ross said seemed beautiful to me. As he spoke, I felt the same sense of comfort and safety that I had sometimes felt in that back room with my father. Now I could put a name to that feeling: it was the Holy Ghost. I told him it was what I wanted, that he was teaching me principles that gave me "somewhere safe" to be. He invited me to come to his church. There was a small branch that met on the nearby American army base. I went, and the peacefulness and lightness I felt there made a great impression on me. The other Church members were welcoming and seemed happy to have this poor, atheistic, former Muslim in their midst. No one asked me what family I came from, what part of Istanbul I grew up in, what political views I held, or any of the other usual questions that defined and labeled members of Turkish society. I was simply accepted as Ayse, with no labels or preconceptions. It was a unique experience.

I was still planning to go to Saudi Arabia to work, and my paperwork was due to go through at any time. I hadn't told Ross about my plans, but one day I felt prompted to call him at home and tell him. When I phoned, he was silent a moment, absorbing this, and then he told me simply, "You can't go."

"Why not?"

"It's too hot there."

"Not hotter than here."

"There are snakes there."

I began to laugh.

He kept naming excuses, all of them silly or unfounded. When he finally ran out of reasons for why I shouldn't go, Ross said, "Ayse, we need to talk. Can you come over?"

This stopped my laughter. I had been invited to the home of a bachelor. That just wasn't done. I had never been to his house. Somehow, going to his home felt different from living in a house full of multiple bachelors. I wasn't sure about it, but I went. I felt I could trust him. I also sensed that this conversation would be more important than the others we had shared.

When I got there, Ross looked solemn and thoughtful. It felt different, standing in his living room alone with him instead of being in a public place surrounded by other people.

He thanked me for coming. Then he said, "Would you like to come to my bedroom? I want to show you something."

Of course, this set off alarm bells in my head, but I looked at his kind face and still felt that he was trustworthy, so I nodded. He led me into the bedroom and went to the bedside table. He took out a little box. Inside it was a ring with a ruby and two diamonds. I didn't know the value of such stones, but it looked expensive.

Ross took my hand, removed Tim's ring from my finger, and put his ring on my finger in its place. Then he said quietly, simply, "Now you can go tell your fiancé you two aren't engaged anymore."

Tears came to my eyes. The tears made the stones in that ring gleam and shimmer brightly. They looked awfully beautiful. We had never spoken of marriage before, but I knew immediately that it was right. So I was engaged to Ross Hitchins. I told Tim, and Ross told Bonnie.

* * *

Happiness is a difficult thing to trust. All my life I'd had it held out to me and then yanked away. Like a hummingbird, it always darted and flitted just out of reach, tantalizing, never landing. Almost everything in my life to that point had been impermanent. I was accustomed to abrupt change; not only had I learned to adapt to it, but I had also learned to expect it at every turn. I felt the good and the beautiful were fragile and would not last, so it was difficult for me to let myself truly feel deep joy or to be hopeful. I was fearful of letting myself be too happy because I thought it would only end in disappointment. I was afraid to go too high for fear of falling. I was sick of being disappointed in life and had built protective barriers around myself. I had grown to feel that I apparently wasn't someone who deserved joy.

Now with this new promise of happiness before me, my nerves were jangling. I was afraid Ross would go back to Canada, forget about me, and never come back. All my life I had waited for things, and I was determined this was one thing that would not slip away from me. I didn't want a long, drawn-out engagement. I wasn't going to sit down and think about it or worry. I didn't want this beautiful chance to dart away and elude my grasp. I told Ross to take me to the Canadian embassy, tell them I was his fiancée, and start the paperwork for me to go to Canada. I had no idea what the process would involve or how long it would take, but I wanted to get started right away.

We went to the embassy, hand in hand, and I felt very excited and proud to be seen on the arm of this handsome Canadian. However, when we arrived, we were told that Ross could only do the application from Canada, not while he was in Turkey. I was very disappointed, and I really struggled against the fear that he would get on the plane, go back to Canada, and forget all about me. Looking back, I can see that this insecurity stemmed from the feeling I had that he could not truly be in love with me. I felt myself basically unlovable, and to trust that this man whom I'd only known a short while could be that invested in me was a foreign concept to me. While I told myself my fears were irrational, they were nonetheless real. I wanted to believe in Ross, but everything in my life to that point had taught me not to believe in other people. It was a real battle within me.

Then, with Ross's encouragement, over the next few weeks I took the discussions with the LDS missionaries. My English was still very poor, but somehow during those lessons with the missionaries, the veil was lifted, I was given clarity of mind, and I was able to understand everything they taught me. The doctrine I learned was beautiful and comforting. They told me I would be able to see my beloved father again, that death did not separate us forever. It was an overwhelming and jolting truth to learn that I was a child of God, of great worth, and that Christ loved me *individually* enough to die for me. I wanted to believe it; I felt it was true. The whole idea was a strange concept to me, but I liked it. What a wonderful feeling to belong to someone. The concepts they taught me were soothing to my soul and nourishing to my heart. I took in the precepts like a starving woman grasping at bread.

As I met with those missionaries, my understanding of gospel principles was enlightened in a way that went beyond the limits of this world. There was no way that, with my limited language skills, I should have been able to grasp these complicated concepts, yet I could. I recognized that some higher power was helping me understand. At first I couldn't name that higher power, but I felt it working within me. I knew the things I was being taught were important, vital, even crucial. I felt I had been waiting a long time to hear them. With my crazy problems regarding age, I may not be able to place myself in *time*, but through those missionary discussions I found my place in *eternity*.

One by one I gained a testimony of the different teachings they presented to me. I had no difficulty accepting the principle of tithing and began paying it right away. Once God told me to do something, I just did it, as simple as that. After much study and prayer, I decided to be baptized into the Church. In my heart, joining the Church was the right thing to do, and I made that decision without any hesitation. I knew exactly what I was getting into when it came to making covenants, thanks to my dad's example. This was not something to fall into lightly; I took it very seriously, with my eyes wide open.

I was introduced to an LDS couple, Marvin and Gay Nell Poulton, who took me in so I was no longer homeless and had no need to stay with my Nigerian friends. The Poultons were Americans working in Turkey, and I stayed with them for several weeks. They already had eight children of their own and were caring for three foster children, but they gave me a place too.

It was my first experience of really living with an ordinary family. All their children looked alike to me, mostly blond, the eldest being about my age (he was on a mission at the time). Brother Poulton was tall and handsome, and his wife was a very lively and very motherly American woman. They treated me like their daughter, and we had many long conversations together. I think they found me intriguing; my life story fascinated them. They were like no one else I had ever met before, and I'm sure they thought the same of me. They valued me as a child of God and treated me like one, and I soaked in the atmosphere of love and acceptance.

It was arranged that I would be baptized and marry Ross on the same day. The night before it was all to happen, Ross came to see me. His face, which had become so dear to me, was downcast, and I knew right away that something was wrong. That beautiful light was missing from his eyes.

He came right to the point. "I don't think we should get married," he said abruptly.

I felt my heart sink. Surely happiness wasn't about to dart away again. I had been so ready to trust it and welcome it this time.

"What happened?" I asked, trying to keep my emotions under control. "Why the sudden change?"

"I'm not sure if this is the right thing for me to do at this time. Things are going very fast," he said.

I knew in my heart these were not his words. I felt that his mother, Lorna Hitchins, who had come from Canada for the wedding, had greatly influenced him because she didn't really approve of our marriage. I worried that Ross's fears were getting the best of him. I also knew that nothing was going to change my mind about my baptism the next morning. With or without Ross, joining the Church was the right decision for me. But I so wanted him to be beside me through this next transition. I was fully committed to both plans—the baptism *and* the marriage.

I opened my mouth to tell him I was still going to be baptized and to tell him how I felt about him, how I wanted to marry him, but before I could say anything, he took his wedding ring from his pocket and held it out to me.

"I'm sorry, Ayse," he said.

I was very sorry too. Here I was on the eve of my biggest day, and things were falling apart right before my eyes.

I tried to keep my voice steady as I told him that, regardless of his decision, I was going ahead with both plans and he was welcome to attend both of them. I also told him I was going to wait for him at the altar because I loved him. As I spoke these words, I found new strength in my heart. I wasn't going to let him go without a fight.

After Ross left, I stood there holding his ring, and I couldn't help but cry. Despite my renewed strength, there was also great sorrow in my heart. I sought out Sister Poulton, who cuddled me in her arms and told me she loved me. It was so comforting to be held by a mother and be gently soothed. But even though her care helped me, I was upset and worried.

"I'm still taking the step to become a Mormon," I told her. "It's still the right path for me."

"Yes. And you know we'll be there for you," she said.

"But what about Ross?" I wailed. "If I can't have Ross, where am I ever going to find another husband in Turkey who is a Latter-day Saint?"

Sister Poulton smiled and said I had no need to worry about such things. Brother Poulton told me to hang in there, do what I knew to be right, and then trust God to take care of the rest. How grateful I was for their friendship and love at a time like this. The Poultons were a great source of comfort to me.

That night was one of the longest of my life. I slept very little. I prayed a lot. At some point during the night, I had a dream that told me all was going to be well and I would feel the complete peace of forgiveness when I was baptized. The feelings from that dream lingered with me when I awoke, and I got out of bed ready to go through with it.

It was very early, and the sun was just coming up. It had been arranged for the baptism to take place in the outdoor pool on the American army base in Ankara. The Poultons accompanied me, and when I arrived, it was a pleasant surprise to see many fellow members there who, despite the early hour, had come to see yet another soul enter the waters of baptism.

And then I saw Ross standing by the pool.

I was overjoyed to see him there. He had come to witness one of the biggest steps of my life. That told me he did love me deeply. It was wonderful to see him smiling at me as if to say, "You are safe in Heavenly Father's care. He loves you as much as I love you, and maybe even more." I could hardly wait to enter into the water. I was so excited and knew I was doing the right thing.

As Brother Poulton took me by the hand and led me down the steps into the swimming pool, for the first time in my whole life, I felt complete peace. The promise of the vision the night before was fulfilled. I knew I was about to be forgiven of all my past sins and that here was my chance to start a new life. All was going to be washed from my body, my soul, and my heart. As I went under the water for those few seconds and came up again, I felt as if time stood still. It was a strange yet unforgettable moment.

I was baptized at six in the morning, June 16, 1984. I remember the water was extremely cold. I will never forget the feelings I had in my heart that morning.

Shortly after my baptism, I wrote these lines in my journal:

June 16, 1984
Dear Heavenly Father,
Today is very special to me. My motherlike friend, Gay Nell Poulton, is helping me with every detail on this special day. Here we are at the swimming pool. Although it is so early in the morning, there are many members and the man I love.

Last night I saw a dream. In my dream, there were two children beside me. The branch president asked one of the little boys to be baptized first, but I wanted to be baptized before anyone else. I was nearly in tears, praying for him to change his mind. All of a sudden, he called my name and asked if I wanted to be the first one. How happy I was to hear him say that. And I woke up.

That is exactly what happened this morning. I could not believe that everything was the same as my dream. My heart was like the wings of a bird, wanting to go free out of my chest. I was so happy but scared. What if I could not keep the promises I made? But I know I am doing the right thing. It is a strange feeling I have. I do know that my baptism will open the temple's door for me. I know Joseph Smith was a prophet and President Kimball is the living prophet today.

With all my heart, I want to see my dad and talk to him again. I want to tell him there is life after death and we will see each other again. I hope I will have a happy marriage and healthy children who will be baptized by Ross.

Dear Lord, I can't explain so many things I am feeling. You know me better than I know myself. Now I am going to take yet another important step. This afternoon I will be married. Please help me to get through all this excitement today. Thanks for all that You have given me. Please always help me and hear my prayers.

I say these things in the name of Jesus Christ. Amen.

After my baptism, I was surrounded by people (including Ross) who gave me big hugs and reassured me that they would be there to help me in any way they could. I believed them too. Just like the other members of The Church of Jesus Christ of Latter-day Saints, I became a follower of Christ. To someone who is Muslim, to understand the concept of Jesus Christ being the Son of God is really difficult if not impossible. But for me, I knew it was true and that from that day on, His Atonement included me as well. It is very difficult to explain how I knew, but I just knew. I also knew that forever and ever this was never going to change. The gospel principles I was learning became a lifeline to me. A mighty change was taking place in my heart. The light of Christ was entering into my soul, and the seeds of tolerance and forgiveness were taking root. My burden was light, and I was set free from the bondage of past sins. Entering into the waters of baptism made all of this possible. How powerful is that?

Today, after twenty-seven years of membership in the Church, I can safely say I am finally beginning to comprehend the significance of the Atonement. I know God lives and loves His children. I know Jesus is the Christ and that He is the Son of the living God. I know this to be the everlasting truth. Even if I were to die for defending the truthfulness of the gospel, I would never take my testimony back, just as I promised. When I made the covenant, I knew what I was doing, and I wasn't going to look back.

Chapter Fourteen

"Be of good cheer, little children; for I am in your midst, and I have not forsaken you."
—Doctrine and Covenants 61:36

I DIDN'T KNOW IF ROSS would show up for our wedding later that day or not, but I went ahead and got ready, determined to carry it out. The reception hall was decorated with wonderful flowers. Sister Poulton had sewn all the bridesmaids' dresses for my fairytale wedding. There was a two-tiered white wedding cake, a gift from the chef. Everything was so beautiful.

The hour drew close. Guests started to arrive. The photographer set up his equipment and stood looking expectant. I asked everyone I knew if Ross had come yet. No one had seen him. I was still confident he was the one for me. I put on my white wedding gown with its long veil and put little flowers in my hair. I held Ross's ring in my hand. And I waited.

Finally, I received word: Ross had come.

I don't have words to describe my relief and happiness. He looked more handsome than ever in his navy blue suit. His smile warmed my heart, and I knew everything was going to be all right. Brother Poulton stood in for my father to give me away, and as I took Ross's hand, I knew we were doing the right thing.

Members of the Ankara branch put together the wedding reception. Many members made this special day possible for both of us, and their selfless act still stands as a testament to me of Christlike charity. It was wonderful to see so many of our friends at our little gathering. Ross's best man was our dear friend, Fred Beasley. He and Ross had been best friends for many years. Ross's father had died many years before, but his mother was there. My dear friend Pelin Ercan was there too. All of her siblings had wanted to come as well, but due to their financial circumstances, they could not. Later on I learned that Pelin actually used her last pennies to buy a bus ticket so she could come to my wedding. Oh, how I love her for that.

I had seen my family occasionally, and they knew there were transitions happening in my life, but I had not told them outright that the Church I was being baptized into was Christian. They may have suspected it, but nothing was ever said. The only person I had at my wedding from my family was my brother, Cihangir. I did not want to see anybody else, only him, at my marriage. After all, he was the only person who should share my joy after sharing so much of my sorrow. We both deserved to share a little bit of happiness. I wished intensely that my father could have been there.

Years later, I learned that Ross's patriarchal blessing told him he would marry a Church member. And so I was, by a matter of hours.

* * *

It was time for Ross to return to Canada; his time in Turkey was over. It took a lot of trust and faith for me to let him get on that plane because even though I knew in my head he wasn't lost to me, that we would be together again, it was hard for my heart to believe it. I found myself constantly rubbing that ring on my finger, like a talisman tying me to this man I astonishingly but unquestioningly had grown so quickly to love.

Once he got home, Ross submitted the paperwork for me to immigrate and eventually join him. But just one week later, Ross's company said his job required more time, and they sent him back to Turkey. We were able to be together again, and I began to think that perhaps this time things were going to work out after all. God had arranged it so Ross could be in Canada long enough to start the paperwork rolling and then return to Turkey, to me. I felt we were being watched over by a benevolent eye.

When I graduated from the university with a music degree in 1983, I had an outstanding student loan of eighty-two thousand old Turkish lira, which was about two hundred and seventy-six US dollars at the time. It seems a paltry sum now, but at the time, it ordinarily would have taken me several years to pay it back. However, Ross and I didn't want to leave the country with a debt over our heads, so we paid the loan off when we left Turkey. I got a 15 percent discount because I paid it in cash. Today you could hardly buy anything with that amount. But at the time, it was a huge amount to me.

On November 17, 1984, I became a landed immigrant. We arrived in Canada by way of Germany, with all my worldly possessions in two suitcases, one of them broken.

* * *

Leaving Turkey. Had I ever really thought I would do it? During all my traveling around the country and dreaming of far-off places, had I ever really believed I would one day go? Everything happened so fast that I suppose I didn't feel much at the time; I had no time to think about it. I landed at the Toronto Pearson International Airport to cold weather and an unfamiliar landscape. Flat countryside. Broad, sixteen-lane-wide, smooth-surfaced highways. Shiny new cars. Colorful brick houses built side by side with garages bigger than our entire house in Karaman. No dirt or rock to be seen. The sky wasn't the rich, clear blue I was used to but was covered in low-lying clouds, turning the sky to buttermilk. I felt I had landed on another planet.

I remember driving through the town of London, Ontario, and seeing a lot of lights; it was close to Christmas, and everything was lit up. I had never seen such a thing before. The plan was for me to stay with Ross's mother in London while Ross was working in Toronto, about two and a half hours away. Because Ross would be busy all day, he thought it best for his mother and me to keep each other company. I had met his mother briefly at the wedding but did not know her well. I knew she hadn't been pleased about our marriage, and I was quite anxious to have her come to like me. I felt I had to prove to her, to everyone, that I was the right girl for Ross—that I could manage this great big change in my life and make Ross happy.

We arrived at his mother's home, and, to my surprise, Mother Hitchins was more British than I'd expected. She had come to Canada from England after World War II. Her proper ways and her lifestyle were overwhelming to me. I admit I might have been a bit rough around the edges, considering the rather vagabond life I had been living recently. I especially had trouble understanding her accent. I had studied English in school and had expected to be able to adapt quickly and communicate without much struggle, but I would listen to Ross's mother speak and think to myself, *Have I had a stroke and not noticed? I should understand this, but I don't.* Above all other challenges, the worst was that she and I couldn't communicate. I wanted to be close to her and had anticipated her being a mother to me, but I was disappointed to learn that just wanting was not enough. I just said yes to everything she said because I couldn't understand her, and I feared offending her in some way. I think she tried to be kind and loving, but the lack of communication was too much for us. It took a toll on both of us, and I became depressed and homesick.

Everything was foreign to me—the food, the clothing, the furnishings, the beautiful bathroom fixtures, the elevator, the weather, the sights and smells and sounds. So many tall, fair, English-speaking people walking around. Even the colors were different in Canada, somehow less intense and vibrant, more brown and earthy. I didn't know how to function in this new world. It was like being dropped into a train station without any signposts or directions. There was nothing familiar I could get ahold of, and I was reliant on someone else for everything, a feeling I was not accustomed to. I couldn't even buy bread by myself. After being so fiercely independent for so long, I found this new mode of being almost suffocating.

One thing I avoided was the No Frills chain grocery store. In order to save money, the company used generic identical packaging for everything. The products were all in uniform yellow, and the only way to tell what was inside was by reading the label on the package. There were no pictures on the front to tell me what was inside, and my English wasn't good enough figure out what was in the particular box or can I was confronting. I found it daunting and humiliating that I couldn't do such a basic thing as shop for my own food. I stuck to fresh vegetables and the meats in the glass counter, where I could point to what I wanted without having to speak. Since then, I have always had a soft spot in my heart for illiterate people. I had to function briefly in their world and found it extremely difficult.

My stomach was homesick as well. I missed the *doner* (gyro sandwich wraps) and kebabs, the sticky baklava and *lokum* (Turkish Delight) with pistachios. I even dreamt of *lahmacun,* a very thin, pizzalike crust with spicy meat on it. Canadian food seemed bland and uninteresting compared to the foods of my youth, and sometimes I wondered if the only herbs and spices Canadians had heard of were salt and pepper. Years later, Ross admitted that the first time he ever kissed me he had badly burned his mouth (I had been eating spicy peppers), and it had caused him serious concern about how our marriage would ever work out. He had been raised on very tame British food, and he wasn't sure he would be able to survive years of my spicy cooking. As he put it, he knew life with me was going to be interesting.

More than ever, I missed my dad. There were nights that I could not sleep because I lay awake thinking of him. Though it was a strange thought, I felt that I had left him behind in Turkey and that he would never be able to find me anymore. I had wandered too far away. This was more than general homesickness. Night after night I prayed to feel his presence once again because I wanted him to know I had made many positive changes in my life and was finally becoming the daughter he deserved to have. I felt the need to be able to communicate that to him. I deeply believed there was a life after this one, and I sensed that somewhere, in some way, Dad was still there and wanting to hear from me, but I was lost and cut off from him.

During one of my heartfelt prayers, I finally felt his presence, as if he were right next to me. I opened my eyes, and there he was. There was no sense of surprise or alarm, only happiness and joy in my heart. As he sat on my bed next to me, he said there was nothing to worry about and that he was watching me every step of the way. He also knew that sooner or later I was going to find the right path and do many good works throughout my life. Tears ran down my cheeks, but I was comforted and at peace. He was here with me. I knew with surety at that moment that my dad was pleased with my choices, and it did not matter where I was; he was going to be with me in my life. That was one of the biggest gifts I have ever received from my Heavenly Father. I thanked Him with all my heart for allowing me to experience the presence of my dad in one of my darkest moments in this strange land.

* * *

During one of Ross's visits home that first Christmas, he had a really bad idea. He suggested one evening that he teach me to pull the car into Mother Hitchins's garage. It was the first time I'd ever sat behind the wheel. He gave me a quick lesson about brakes, gas pedals, and the automatic transmission and then said, "You'll do fine."

I took this as my signal, not stopping to think, of course, that the driver's door was still open and Ross was half in and half out of the car. I stomped down hard on the gas, and the car shot forward. Ross yelled, and the engine screamed as he, hopping on one foot, tried to hit the brake. The open car door hit the left side of the garage, crushing Ross in the process. Somehow, in all the pandemonium, we managed not to shoot the car through the garage wall into Mother Hitchins's kitchen. Ross berated me, and I protested that I hadn't understood and he was a lousy teacher and I was not impressed with his tutelage. Ross went into the kitchen afterward and found his mother standing at the sink, which was on the opposite side of the garage wall. She was standing directly in the path of the car, had it gone through the wall.

Things went from bad to worse with the relationship between Mother Hitchins and me after that. After about a month of war, I finally phoned Ross.

"I can't do it any more," I told him. "It is too hard on your mother. She tries so hard, and it's no good."

Ross didn't argue or hesitate. He drove to London and picked me up (still with my two pathetic suitcases) and took me to Toronto. We lived with Ross's good friends, Brother and Sister Gernon, who were members of the Church. They were extremely kind and accommodating and tried their best to make me feel welcome in their home. I will always cherish their love and friendship. It felt better being with Ross, being able to see him when he returned from work each evening, and I didn't feel quite so lost.

Ross also took this opportunity to teach me something important: in this culture it was okay to speak back to an older person, to ask for them to repeat themselves or say things more slowly or in a different way so I could understand them. He told me it was all right for me to disagree and speak up; I didn't have to say yes to everything. Saying yes to everything could lead to trouble. It was a valuable lesson to learn.

It was a period of intense learning. There was so much to grasp. When you're learning a different language, there is a delay in your brain between what you hear and what you process. People would tell me jokes in English, and ten minutes after everyone else had finished laughing, I would get it and laugh aloud. The delayed reaction would spark more laughter. I also found that people would shout at me, as if I were deaf or stupid, thinking that if they were louder, somehow I would understand better.

As a newcomer to North America, I also ran into an attitude of "us versus you." People were convinced that my side of the world was not worth mentioning and their side of the world was the greatest. Coming from a place with a six-thousand-year-old history, I used to mutter to myself, "What do you know? Your country is only two hundred years old."

However, not everyone treated me that way. There were many wonderful people who gave of themselves in my life, and I am very grateful for them. Once before coming to Canada, Ross and I attended a dinner in Ankara. There, I met a very nice gentleman named John. He was very high up in Ross's company, but I didn't know enough English to understand ranks or positions. I only knew that this nice man was Ross's boss. That night at dinner I kept John company. He was going to visit Istanbul, and we arranged for me to go along to be his tour guide. We planned to spend the better part of a day together in the city. He told me I was very kind and that he really appreciated my hospitality. He said to me then, "If you ever come to Canada, please be my guest and come and visit me."

Soon after we went to Toronto, I announced to Ross that I wanted to go visit John at his house. When we arrived, I realized John must be a wealthy, well-educated man, far more important than I had realized. He had a beautiful, big home made entirely of glass at the Harbourfront with a splendid view of Lake Ontario. It turned out that John had been an engineer for NASA, and he showed me drawings of the projects he had done for them.

His wife cooked us a nice dinner that night. As we were eating, John leaned toward me and said, "I enjoy your company, Ayse."

"Why is that?" I asked.

"Because you treat me like a friend. You value me as a person and not for the position I hold."

I shrugged. "I don't *know* what position you hold," I replied.

This made him laugh. I thought to myself, *What a nice man.* So I leaned over and told him, "If I ever have a child one day, I would really like to name him John."

Slowly I began to learn how to function in this bewildering new land. I made some friends. I learned about traffic rules and the bus system so I could get around more easily without having to rely on others for a ride. I learned enough English to read labels and grocery shop and get my hair cut. I figured out the money and banking system. I began to understand more of what was spoken in church, and I was able to exchange greetings with people I met and start to make acquaintance with the neighbors. I got to the point that I could read newspapers and understand simple children's shows on television, and I started to study the government structure and follow local political issues. I found a doctor and dentist. And I bought a great big map book showing the town in detail so I could find my way around.

"I can do this," I told myself with relief. "I can figure out this country Canada."

A month later Ross was assigned to work in the United States.

* * *

His United States assignment began what I call our "nomad years." We packed our old Volvo with our ten-inch TV and a few clothes and traveled throughout the U.S., with Ross being assigned different technical consulting jobs here and there. For a few months we moved about and lived in hotels and motels. Things were challenging at times, but we were very happy. Ross and I could live in a tent and still be happy. He loved me, and I loved him. Nothing else seemed more important. I felt so fortunate to have him in my life; he was so supportive of my culture and my traditions. I was talking to him about my past once and mentioned my promise to God never to steal anything again after that terrible incident in university. I told him I was proud that I had never broken that promise since that time.

"But you did break your promise," Ross replied.

"No, I never stole anything again," I insisted.

"Yes, you did," he told me. "You stole my heart."

Do you wonder why I would follow such a man across the globe?

Our frequent moving did limit my ability to make friends. It seemed I had hardly introduced myself to people at church and learned a few names before it was time to pack up and go again. Because we were not able to put down roots or really form a social network at the beginning,

Ross and I had to rely on each other a great deal, and I think this was a good way to start our marriage.

I still struggled with my English, having a limited vocabulary, and I was afraid of getting lost and not being able to communicate well enough to find my way home again. This was especially true because we really didn't live in one place long enough to get to know the area. Whenever I walked to the grocery store, I would take a piece of chalk and mark big *X*s on objects—trees, signposts, brick walls—so I could follow them back home, like Hansel and Gretel leaving crumbs in the forest. It was silly, I suppose, but it gave me a sense of security, and it worked. I walked along making my *X* marks and thought, *Here I am, a university graduate, and I feel like an idiot.*

I learned a lot of English from television. I would repeat what I heard, and in the evening I would proudly meet Ross at the door with something like, "American Express . . . Don't leave home without it."

One evening when he came home, I met him at the door in a panic, saying urgently, "I need a scuba diver."

That stopped him in his tracks.

"A what?"

"A scuba diver."

"What on earth do you need a scuba diver for?" he asked.

"For the door," I explained.

Ross shook his head. "I don't understand what you mean."

I tried to control my frustration. "You know, the thing you turn with a handle," I insisted, pantomiming.

"Ahh!" The light went on. "You need a screw driver."

"Yes, that. Whatever," I said.

Over the years, Ross learned to read my mind. I had only to say, "Go get that thing," and somehow he knew just what the "thing" was. Perhaps the Spirit helps us in our marriages more than we know or care to admit. Ross has told me that even though the English language does not come easily to me, when I speak, love and understanding come through my speech from my heart and touch other people's hearts so they understand what I am trying to say. That has been the greatest encouragement I could ever hear.

As my communication skills improved, my confidence increased, and I wanted to regain some of my old independence. I was ready to strike out a little more on my own. I decided the best way to increase my self-reliance was to learn to drive a car. I knew that Ross was too nervous now to be a good driving instructor and insisted I have a professional teacher. It was a wise decision and might possibly have saved our marriage. Even Ross admitted that the female instructor was amazingly calm. One day Ross went out driving with us, and he spent the whole time in the backseat burying his fingertips in the door handle and pounding his foot on an imaginary brake.

I seemed to familiarize myself with a city better once I drove in it. Driving gave me a great sense of freedom, and even today, after years of driving a car, I feel most free when I'm on the road and in control. The traffic didn't bother me at all, and often I spent driving time having little heart-to-heart talks with God. The long drives gave me the chance to unload my burdens on the Lord and seek direction from Him.

* * *

One day, when we were traveling in Tennessee, we lost our minds and bought a little black dwarf bunny that I named Ayten. She was the smallest of the litter, and I suppose I related to her instantly because I was so small myself. She was a wonderful, good-natured animal that brought a lot of joy to our lives, and we quickly grew attached to her. She was domesticated and would spend hours outside her cage socializing with us. Ross had recently been assigned to work in Salisbury, Maryland, and we lived in a motel for three or four weeks while we were looking for a house to rent. On the day we were to move, we couldn't find Ayten.

I was devastated at the thought that we might have to leave without my little rabbit friend. I couldn't stop crying, worried that she had somehow left the motel room through an open door without us noticing. Ross searched the fields surrounding the motel for hours without success. Finally, he came back and told me he had been prompted to return to our motel room. He went straight over to the dresser and pulled all the drawers out, and when he reached the bottom drawer, out popped Ayten's little head. I was so happy that my tears changed to tears of joy instead of sorrow. The little animal must have gotten behind the dresser somehow and wiggled herself into that drawer from the back. Ross laughed pretty hard. I laughed too, but I still cried at the same time. I think once you have experienced deep loss, even small losses can cut deeply and leave you shaken.

Salisbury was a longer-term assignment, enabling us to live there for two years. We lived in a lovely old home with a root cellar on North Park Drive. The house was located right across from the city zoo, which made me happy. I have always enjoyed animals and nature, seeing in them the love God has for His children and the great care He provides for us. I have a soft spot in my heart for the smallest of Heavenly Father's creatures.

We had a lot of fun feeding the ducks almost daily, and there was an old monkey we loved to visit regularly. He was a unique character and loved peanuts. He was used to visitors feeding him, and if you gave him something he didn't like, he would dump the unwanted food petulantly on the ground and hold out his hand once again for something he liked. The funny thing was, he would do this while his gaze was turned elsewhere, as if to say, "I am sassy, and I don't care. Give to me if you like; I'm not invested in it one way or the other." And who could argue with such a cute monkey?

There were also a number of animals living in our backyard, which provided hours of entertainment for us. One of these creatures was an opossum that played dead on the tree. It was one of the funniest things I had ever seen. There he was, lying on his back on the tree trunk, one eye closed, one eye opened, playing dead while watching us to make sure we believed he was dead. He didn't realize that wanting something didn't make it true. Oh my goodness, it was a funny scene. Ross went outside with a flashlight to investigate, and as he drew closer and closer to this cute creature, we could see the opossum's one eye shining red in the dark. We both laughed out loud. What a smart animal.

Another lovely animal friend was a little chipmunk. He loved stuffing his face with seeds and nuts, and he never understood my explanation that there was plenty for all and that he didn't need to worry about being deprived tomorrow.

There was a squirrel we called Mama who became so accustomed to our feeding her that when we left our screen door open, she would come right inside the house to find us. She would sit looking at us very pointedly until we acknowledged it was feeding time. One Christmas, Mama came into the house and saw the artificial Christmas tree in our living room. She studied it carefully and then apparently decided that any home with a tree in it was her territory too. She started hiding nuts amongst the presents under the tree and in our potted plants.

We had a wonderful time in our backyard, enjoying all of God's beautiful creations. The natural habitat in Salisbury was very different from Turkey's. It was not easy to explore the natural world that closely in a big city like Istanbul, where the only animals we were likely to encounter were pigeons.

Ayten also loved grazing in the yard, even at night. Her little red eyes would light up like two red rubies in the dark. What was really fascinating was that Ayten became good friends with our neighbor Mrs. Hastings's dog. The big dog and the little bunny had a unique bond. The dog protected his new friend fiercely and would not let anyone come near her. Their friendship strengthened my love for God's creations. One does not need to go far to find miracles.

* * *

Ross worked eleven- or twelve-hour night shifts at Salisbury airport, and I found a job forty-five miles away as a waitress in a restaurant. I dropped him off, worked until one in the morning in the restaurant, then went to a pizza parlor the restaurant owner also owned, where I worked until four in the morning making pizzas. Then I would drive the forty-five miles back to pick up Ross from his work and be home by five in the morning. I would bring home food from the restaurant, and we would eat and count the tips I'd collected in my apron (on average, one hundred dollars a night). Then we would sleep. We did this all summer and had enough money by September to go on a ten-day cruise to the Caribbean. The name of the ship was the *Sun Viking*, and we had the best vacation. We cheerfully spent every dime I had made.

Ross then switched to a day job, so I switched too. I started working as a volunteer in a hospital three or four times a week. That was much easier than working at night. I hadn't realized how much I had missed being part of the bustling daytime world, how much I had missed the sunlight on my skin.

I felt that each day was a gift from God. But it was not all sunshine and roses. Though Ross and I had fallen for each other quickly and deeply, it was still a challenge to bring two completely different people together in a marriage. For the first couple of years, we fought fiercely. I think we packed ten years' worth of arguments into two. Because of our language barriers, we had our own unique style: we fought with dictionaries. He would say something (for example: "That's rubbish"), and I would hold up a hand and say, "Wait!" I'd look up *rubbish* in the dictionary. When I found out what it meant, I'd fling back, "How can you say that's garbage?" Then I'd say something, and he'd say, "Wait!" and look it up in his Turkish dictionary. Of course, having to pause so often inevitably took the fire out of things. After a while, the ridiculousness of the situation had us both laughing.

I had to teach Ross *how* to fight, initially. He came from a home where his parents had never raised their voices or argued. It just didn't happen. He wanted that same harmonious, loving relationship in his own marriage. Whenever I picked a fight with him, he was uncomfortable with it. One night he asked me, "Why do you always want to fight? My parents never fought."

"That is all I know a married couple should do," I replied. "That is how my parents lived their life."

I could tell that shocked him. "But why should *we* fight?" he asked.

"I don't think you care if you aren't willing to fight or argue," I replied.

Years later, Ross admitted he had thought it a bit silly at the time, but he set about learning to argue, smiling to himself inside as he worked to fight with me a little bit. Anything to keep me happy.

Sometimes the fights were in earnest. Above all, we were politically opposed. I remained a staunch Communist, and Ross was much more conservative. We were our own mini United Nations; Ross represented Canada, and I represented Turkey. When we fought, we exerted our patriotism with great fervor. We had emotion, the national anthem, the flag, everything "flying high." I was—and am—an intense sort of person, and I recall one particularly furious battle when I decided I'd had enough.

"I'm leaving!" I said and started down the hall toward the door. But I didn't get that far. I fell to my knees and began to sob. I was so angry I could hardly speak. It was Karaman, and I was a teenager all over again. "I have no place to go," I choked. "This is not my country."

Of course, Ross rushed to comfort me, the battle forgotten immediately, and we quickly reconciled our differences. Our fights were white-hot, but they didn't last long.

* * *

It had always been our goal to be sealed together as husband and wife, and we were finally able to do this in the Washington DC Temple, that beautiful building that rises like a wedding cake above its reflecting pool. It occurred to me as we drove up to the temple that this building, too, had six spires, like the Blue Mosque's minarets. As I had once oriented myself with the Mosque, I now had a new building in the center of my life, a new place by which to orient myself and from which to take direction. The temple anchored me so I never wandered and was lost again.

Several friends attended our sealing, including the Poultons, who had returned from Turkey. It felt right to me to finally be sealed forever to Ross. *This* was something no one and nothing could take away from me now, not even death. This was one happiness that could not flit away like that uncatchable hummingbird. This was the way things were supposed to be, I felt, and my convictions of the truth of the gospel grew even stronger.

Ross was a very patient and kind person. He was grounded, and that helped me learn to be grounded as well (which was good, because initially, I was all over the place). He would express his own ideas, stand up for them, and not let others trample them, including me. But he always let me be free. That was one of the things about him I most valued. He never prohibited me from taking my own path and exploring new ideas but always supported and encouraged me. He was the epitome of the admonishment in Doctrine and Covenants 121 to exercise the priesthood in righteousness, with longsuffering, gentleness, and love unfeigned. Though I believed I loved him deeply at the time I married him, I look back on it from a quarter of a century further down the road, and I can see I hardly knew the meaning of the word then. It can't be compared to the love I feel for him now. He is the love of my life. In my journal I once recorded:

How wonderful it is to gather around the kitchen and talk about our daily life with one another. We will not remember what we ate, but we will always remember the wonderful feeling of being an eternal family.

Ross came from such a different background from mine. He grew up loving his family and knowing his parents loved him, something he never felt he had to question. These people just assumed they would always be there for each other. Even though he had lost his father to cancer at a young age, he grew up knowing the security of the bond they'd shared. Through watching his example, I began to value family life. He inspired me to reevaluate what I felt for my own family. In a way, he gave me ownership of my relationship with them.

Ross and I looked forward to having a family of our own, but things did not happen according to plan. After some time, we learned that having children would not be an option for us. It was very disappointing, and for a time, it felt as if the bottom had dropped out of our world. Was this happiness going to be withheld too, after everything else, just when life was finally going right? Surely having a family was a righteous desire. Why would that be denied us?

But, of course, I have never been one to take no for an answer. We looked at various paths we might take, weighed our options, and decided to adopt. It felt like the right decision for us. However, we were told we couldn't adopt in Maryland because we were Canadians, and we couldn't adopt through Canada because we were living in the States. We decided it was time to move back to Canada.

Adoption was our primary reason for moving, but shortly after we returned to London, Ontario, we learned that Ross's mother also had cancer. It saddened me to see the challenges this gentle woman faced, and we were glad to be nearby so we could spend time with her. She and I could finally communicate better. Ross and I developed the habit of going to her home for Sunday dinner after church, and we would play Scrabble together for a couple of hours. The game built our relationship and my language skills at the same time. I took a beating at that game every Sunday for two years, and then one evening I won. Ross was very proud of me, and I suspected he and his mother had let me win, but Ross insisted it wasn't true. I had beaten them, fair and square.

Games were something new to me. I had never played games as a child, and the concept was foreign to me. I couldn't see the point of board games, for the most part. Early in our marriage, Ross brought home a game of Monopoly and walked me through it once, explaining the perplexing concepts. Then we went at it, and he made me go bankrupt. Of course, Ross was gleeful about that, but I was disgusted with the whole thing.

"This is a stupid Capitalist game," I said with all the fervor of my Communist upbringing. I scooped up all the pieces and money and tore them up, flinging them into Ross's lap.

I didn't realize at the time how much this hurt his feelings. Ross was totally crushed at how his introduction to games had gone over. He later told me he believed one of the reasons I loved the gospel so much was the law of consecration. He could tell it was a concept dear to my heart. He had understood I hadn't just been angry about losing the silly game; it was the injustice of one person having dominion over another, making them go bankrupt, that rubbed me wrong. Having someone lose without someone helping them out was just not right. I later found out that Ross kept the pieces of the ruined game to remind himself of that.

Ross's mother challenged me a lot; though she meant well, some of what she said provoked me. Sometimes she said, "You could never make it in a university here." It was hurtful to me at the time, but I see now that she was really trying to push me into going back to school. She knew I was not one to take a challenge lying down. I had not lost my thirst for education, and even though I had been learning at a rapid rate since immigrating, I still craved formal schooling. I wanted to prove Ross's mother wrong. I decided my English skills were good enough that I could understand classroom lectures, and in September 1986, I began attending the University of Western Ontario full time to obtain a degree in sociology.

I have found that people tend to form a picture of themselves in their heads, and anything that doesn't fit that picture causes them distress. They end up either denying the thing that doesn't fit or fighting to change the thing so it will fit; rarely do they opt simply to change the image they have of themselves. I had been an A student in Turkey, and that was the image I had of myself: capable and intelligent. But my new life in Canada challenged that self-image. My first year at the university in Canada, I got a C in one of my courses, and I was inconsolable. I knew I could do better than that, and it spurred me on to try harder. I fought to maintain the image I had of myself. Eventually my grades climbed, and I no longer bawled over my test scores. But it was a real challenge to my ego for a while.

During this time, my brother Cihangir, who was about eighteen or nineteen years old, asked if he could come to Canada and live with us. He hoped to find better opportunities for himself in a new country. Ross and I talked it over and agreed. In many ways, I still felt like a mother to

Cihangir, and I was happy to have him come. I knew he had had difficulty holding a job in Turkey, and his life wasn't following a good path at the time. I was eager to open new opportunities to him, to show him all the things I had learned and share with him all the new experiences I was having. Like myself, he needed to start over in a new place.

Life settled into a busy but functional routine. Cihangir went through many of the same struggles I had gone through to adapt to this new land, but I was able to soften it for him because I was there to translate. I hadn't had anyone to translate for me. He learned enough of the language and culture that he was able to find work. He didn't understand or necessarily agree with our LDS lifestyle, but we all did our best to be patient and to make allowances for each other. It took some adapting to have this person who was on the cusp of adulthood but not quite there yet in our home.

During that time I was in school full time, and Ross worked full time. We had filed the paperwork for adoption, but it was a long and slow process. Sometimes it felt purely hypothetical, as if it would never happen. I had learned not to hope for it too much for fear of disappointment. Then one day in early 1988, Ross and I had an argument about who would watch the baby if and when we did finally manage to adopt. I don't recall what triggered the fight, but it was clear we were both busy and equally dedicated to what we were doing. A child would require time and flexibility. Who was going to give?

The artillery was ready to come out again, dictionaries and all, but right in the middle of the argument, the phone rang. I answered it.

"Sister Hitchins? This is Brother Barber from LDS Social Services."

I froze and looked at Ross, wide-eyed, suddenly unable to speak. He could see my reaction and bent his head to mine to put his ear near the phone.

We both heard Brother Barber say simply, "We have a child for you. He's six weeks old. He's in Calgary. How soon can you get there?"

We put the argument on hold.

Section Four
New Journeys

Chapter Fifteen

"For this child I prayed; and the Lord hath given
me my petition which I asked of him."
—*1 Samuel 1:27*

THE BABY BOY HAD BEEN born November 30, 1987. Ross and I flew to Calgary, Alberta, in February and, following the directions we'd been given, went to the foster home where the baby was being cared for. A Japanese woman lived there with her husband and four children. I stood beside Ross in the lovely living room of her home and felt lightheaded with eagerness and anxiety. All the way to Alberta, I had chattered like a nervous monkey, but now that the moment was upon me and I was actually there, I felt tongue-tied.

The woman was very friendly and nice, but I don't even recall her name now. I was too stressed to take much in. After speaking to us for a few minutes, the woman left the room and returned a moment later with a blanket-wrapped bundle.

"We call him Buddy," she said with a little shrug and smile.

A hush seemed to fall over the room, and I nearly forgot to breathe. A little round head, like a peach, stuck out from the blanket, with large, staring eyes, and we contemplated each other. That was the first time Ross and I met our son. It was an overwhelming feeling. *Our son.* This little baby was to be ours.

We visited for a long while, gently exploring him, holding him, marveling at him. There was a surreal sense to it because we had waited so long for this moment, and now it was finally here. I've heard other women who have given birth say that, to a degree, they got to know their children's personalities before they were born. This sense of individuality went beyond just being able to tell when the babies woke and slept in the womb, responded to touch or sound, stretched or startled. They felt the babies had patience or impatience, a calm or aggressive nature, which carried on after birth. We hadn't had that opportunity with our son, and yet there was a definite sense of recognition. I found myself thinking, *Yes, this is him.*

We decided we would name him John—a good, strong name—after Ross's boss and after another long-awaited child in the Bible. His name was also a good name for my parents to pronounce in Turkish. In a sort of stupor, we went back to our hotel for the night. I hated to leave him with the foster home for even that short time, but we had no way of caring for him at the hotel. The next morning when we awoke though, we looked at each other and both knew we couldn't do without him, so we went back to the foster home, collected our son, and went back to the hotel.

That night, Ross and I listened to the baby's quiet, gentle breathing, and it was just wonderful to see this little being who was going to be ours forever. In the middle of the night, we touched his soft earlobe to wake him up to feed him (I thought he'd die of hunger if I didn't feed him during the night, but the doctor later set me straight on that score). John was so tiny he just fell into the snowsuit we put on him.

While we were still in Calgary, we attended church in a local ward. After the meetings were over, Ross and I remained seated on our bench in the chapel. John was in a basket beside us. The whole time we had been in Calgary, I had been excited and overwhelmed. But now, as I sat still and quiet there in the empty chapel that Sunday, the full impact of events started to catch up with me. For several years we had dreamt of adopting a child. Now he was here, precious and vulnerable. I wasn't prepared for the attack of emotions I underwent. I had anticipated a certain amount of nervousness or uncertainty at first; that was only natural. But I hadn't anticipated the blast of outright fear that filled me. My hands shook. With something close to terror, I realized I didn't know how to love a child. In that moment, I believed I didn't know how to love anyone. How could I not have foreseen this? I felt terribly inadequate and afraid that I couldn't take care of him. He seemed so incredibly delicate and impossibly reliant on me. What did I know about being a mother? I had never known what a loving mother was, and I felt I had no strong example to fall back on. I'd had substitute mothers, women who had filled in in some ways when I was much older, but right at the very core, as a child, I had not known the love of a mother. I feared I would make all the mistakes Turkan and Fatma had. I would fail John. Above all, I didn't want to fail him.

"Ross, I don't think I can do this," I said, my voice rising in that empty chapel. "This was a mistake. We have to take him back." I began to cry.

"What?" Ross jerked, startled.

"We have to take John back. It's for his own good."

His face went slack. "What are you talking about?"

Between sobs, I tried to explain what I was feeling. I could feel the hysteria rising inside me as I poured out all my doubts and worries. What had I been thinking, taking on this innocent baby? He didn't even know what he was in for.

"I don't even love myself," I wailed. "How am I going to love this child? What am I going to give him? How am I going to raise him?"

Ross was wise and patient. He heard me out until I finally fell silent, and then he held my hand and said sincerely, "You are going to be a great mother. You have so much compassion and love to share. It will come naturally to you."

"You had great parents," I replied. "You know what to do. I don't."

"Ayse," Ross said gently, "I don't know how to be a father either; it's all new to me too. But we'll manage. We will take it one day at a time. We are a covenant-making people. We will raise this child as our own, day by day, precept upon precept. We will *learn* to love him, and I promise I will be here to help you every step of the way."

I trusted him completely when he said he was going to be there to raise this child with me. I looked into his sincere face and knew I wasn't going to be alone. But it still took a great deal of faith.

We kept John, of course. We flew home to Ontario, and Ross gave the baby a name and a blessing: John Bryant Hitchins. The name Bryant came from the ever-helpful, kind, and caring social worker who arranged the adoption. After all these years, we still have a wonderful relationship with him.

Over time I came to grips with it all. Of course I was capable of loving this child. I couldn't help myself; he simply made love pour out of me, an intense warmth of feeling like nothing I'd ever felt before. How could I have doubted? I could trust God to guide me in the raising of this perfect little boy. After all, he was His son too. As time went on, I came to better understand the scripture in 1 John 4:18 that says, "There is no fear in love; but perfect love casteth out fear."

And there the story truly begins.

* * *

When we first brought John home to London, I was in the middle of taking final exams at school. I was studying like mad and trying to get used to having a baby. Ross worked nights, so I was on my own a lot, and it was a trial to keep John quiet during the day so Ross could sleep. We didn't have a crib, so we put John in a drawer lined with pillows. In fact, we didn't have much of anything for the baby. Ross's mother, Lorna, and sister, Sarah, were thrilled and rushed out to buy whatever John needed and more. The ward also had a baby shower for us, and people I hardly knew brought a mountain of gifts. Seeing this gave me confidence because I realized I wasn't alone. I began to believe I could do this. Being surrounded by loving people made a big difference.

I dropped to part-time school and took the baby to classes with me, and no one ever complained. In fact, some teachers, like Dr. Anton Allahar, went out of their way to help me whenever I needed extra help. Just like my music teacher in the past, Dr. Allahar became a great positive influence in my life. He often challenged my mind to overcome limitations and think in new ways. It was a privilege to be his student. He was truly an all-around good teacher, and it was no wonder to me his students at the University of Western Ontario voted him "Best Teacher" several times throughout his career. Right from the beginning, his wife, Anne, and his lovely daughter, Aniisa, loved our son, John. Dr. Allahar nicknamed him "Patrick," though I'm not sure why, but it was an endearment and gave me a warm feeling when he used it. Taking an infant to classes with me was never easy, but we all managed.

There were then, and still are, various schools of thought about how to raise adopted children and how much and when to tell them about their beginnings. There was no debate in my mind about it. We told John from the very first that he was adopted. I wanted no secrets; I didn't want him to find out years later and have his trust shattered, as it had been for me. It was far better to be honest, and it allowed me to explain to him as he was growing up how very much he was anticipated and wanted. He hadn't just happened—he had been *sought out.* We had waited for him for so long. It struck me as meaningful, somehow, that I, as an adopted daughter of an adopted daughter, had now adopted a child of my own, and I wanted him to know about that legacy in his family. (I also joked that if he grew up to adopt a child himself, I was going to call the *Guinness Book of World Records.*)

It had taken Ross and me several years to really know each other because of the communication barrier. But after John's arrival, our focus immediately changed. Our perspectives widened. I truly think parenthood teaches you things you can learn in no other way. It changes your entire outlook on the world.

Life became very busy. In addition to caring for John and going to school, caring for our home, and watching over my brother, I also spent twenty-five hours a week volunteering at hospitals or Church activities or projects. Ross's work kept him traveling one hundred eighty-five days a year, and he was also the bishop of our ward, so I was essentially the one who raised John that first while.

Raising John like I was a single mother was not an easy task. Day after day, week after week, looking after my little one—and Cihangir—took its toll on me. It was more than normal new-mother exhaustion. In fact, my old depression was slowly returning. The old feelings of insecurity and inadequacy began to surface once again. I felt empty and worn out.

When I recognized what was happening, I panicked. I didn't want this to happen, not now when things were going so well and according to plan. I tried my best to act normal during the day so John would be well cared for, but at night I let myself go. I cried many nights and pled with the Lord to help me have strength. I began to feel completely alone and overwhelmed. All I knew was that this little child was totally dependent on me, and I had to play a balancing act for my little baby.

For a while my balancing act worked, and Ross didn't notice my depression. After all, he was struggling with work, travels, and new fatherhood himself. How could I ask him for help when he had so much on his own plate? However, as time went on, I became worse. Naturally, the acting couldn't last long, and I couldn't hide how I felt anymore. One day I found myself in the tight grip of severe depression. This time there was no way out for me.

"What's wrong, Ayse?" Ross asked. "Is there anything I can do for you?" He was so kind and loving, but this was out of his league.

"I don't know what is happening to me," I said, and that was the honest truth. All I knew was I was desolate. I couldn't put my finger on the problem, and I didn't know how to help myself. My own words chilled me; they were what my mother Turkan used to say, "I don't know what is happening to me." A small part of me cowered in the back of my mind, terrified at the thought that I was becoming like her. She was not my mother by birth, but she was my half aunt, and I worried about the genetics I might have inherited. Of course, this worry only intensified my problems.

"I love you, my sweetheart. You mean the world to me," Ross said, wiping the tears from my cheeks with his thumbs.

"How can you love me when I don't even love myself?" I replied.

"Everything will be okay; you will see."

I could not be consoled. "Nothing will be okay," I retorted. "Nothing is ever okay in my life. Whenever I am feeling a little happy, it all goes away again, as if I don't *deserve* happiness."

"Of course you deserve happiness. You are a child of God, and He wants you to be happy. He feels toward you just as you do toward John. Don't you want John's happiness?"

"Of course I do," I answered. "But I don't know if I am even capable of happiness, I really don't. I've never been able to hold on to it. It is all just too hard."

"God gives us trials so our weaknesses can turn into strengths," Ross said.

"I don't feel very strong right now," was my reply. "I am failing as a mother, and I am failing as a wife."

No matter what he said, I found an argument or defense against it. Oh, how terrible was the feeling of being a failure. My heart was full of anxiety, my brain racing ninety miles an hour with unanswered questions and paranoia. I couldn't pinpoint any one problem that vexed me; it was as if all the small questions in my life formed together into one great boulder to crush me. Was there ever going to be enough time in this world for me to learn to be a good mother and a good wife? If I didn't progress fast enough, would God lose patience with me and give up, leave me floundering on my own? What if, in spite of what he promised, Ross left me one day, and I was all alone? Though I knew I wasn't being rational, I still couldn't stop the fearful thoughts from cycling through my head. I was especially afraid of losing Ross. Being alone terrified me. I often saw myself as a little child walking on a very dark road all by myself. Nobody was there to walk with me or to hold my hand. It was just me, going down the never-ending road alone. Since my entrance into the boarding school as a child, I had lived with this image in my head, and now it was emerging once again with full force. My mind often wandered fearfully to the days I had spent in the mental institution, and I wondered if I really was going crazy. All my suppressed feelings rushed to my brain and paralyzed me to the core.

This period of time felt different from my earlier bouts with depression in high school and university. I was on the brink of believing that my world was collapsing and that I would never be able to pull myself out of the rubble. It was at that point that I realized what I was saying to myself: *I couldn't pull myself out. But God could.* I had asked Him for help, but had I really placed myself in His hands? For the past several years, I had learned about God's love for me as an individual. I had studied about the Atonement and the love of Christ, and I felt what I had learned had been more than an intellectual exercise; I had a deep testimony of the concepts. I needed to put them more fully into practice. I knew I needed to go even deeper, to really feel it, to accept that I truly was a loved daughter of God and to let that concept change my life. Until I did that, I didn't really feel I could let God help me.

I think to that point there had still been a bit of resistance on my part: yes, God loved me, but only because He loved everybody, and He would help me because He helped everybody. It was just His nature, nothing to do with me or with my worth. Perhaps He even loved other people *more*—the more worthy, more deserving, more lovable people. Even though I knew I had been forgiven of my sins at baptism, I still felt on some level unworthy, unlovable, and unsaveable. I had reached one level in my progression, but it was time to go deeper. It was time to let Him help *me* as an individual.

Someone once told me that Christ was my salvation, my sanctuary, and my solace. That phrase really struck me. My salvation, yes. I had known that since my baptism. My sanctuary? Yes, in times of struggle, I knew what it meant to take refuge in Christ and His teachings. But my solace? To me, that added a different dimension to everything. It implied comfort, care, and consolation. It was personal, not general.

I embarked on a renewed commitment to prayer and tried hard to let go of my reliance on myself and place myself fully and trustingly in God's hands. For someone used to fighting for everything she got in life, it was a scary thing to stop struggling and let God take over the fight. I gained a new understanding of the meaning of the words *a change of heart, a rebirth*. If I could only let this new understanding work within me, things could and would change. I gained a new appreciation and gratitude for the priesthood holder in my home who was able to give me blessings when I needed them. I recognized the little moments of grace in my life and opened myself to them. And I began to feel better. A small light began to grow in the darkness.

I also went several times to visit my family doctor. Over time I learned that even mothers who do not give birth can suffer from postpartum depression, and that was a great part of what I was suffering from. I may not have had the same hormonal changes of a woman who had given birth, but I still had the emotional changes, which could affect chemical reactions within me. Once I was able to identify and name my ailment, I was better able to face what was happening to me.

It took me almost a year to completely recover, and it was a very humbling experience. I had to rely on Christ and trust Him to help me when I couldn't help myself. During this time, I learned to watch for the tender mercies God offered and recognize the moments when He carried me through my trials. I learned to lean on the arm of the Lord and let Him heal my heart and soul. The fiery furnace of the Lord was at work, trying to create yet another masterpiece, and I had to humble myself, step back, and let it work.

* * *

When I first came to Canada, I vowed I would never return to Turkey. I had too many harsh feelings for my family, especially Turkan. Ross told me that one day I would regret that decision, so after much debate, Ross and I went home to Karaman in 1989. It felt strange to return, to go back as part of a couple now instead of on my own, to return as a parent instead of a child. My parents were polite to Ross but clearly viewed him as something exotic and strange. They weren't sure what to make of this blue-eyed Canadian. We stayed with my parents for only one night. I wasn't sure what Ross would think of their little house—the sleeping on the floor, the eating from a communal pot. He handled it very graciously, and everyone behaved, but it was still a very awkward stay, and I didn't sleep the entire night. I could only lie there thinking, *Hopefully the dawn will break soon and I can get out of here.*

John, a toddler at the time, was with us. As I tossed and turned and stared into the dark, I began to think about my son and how I felt about him. I thought of what I wanted for him and how much his health and happiness meant to me. During that long, miserable night, I began to realize I didn't have to be like my parents. I didn't have to make the mistakes Turkan and Fatma had made. I wasn't going to be them; I could change things. My son didn't have to go through the madness I'd gone through as an adopted child. I began to see within a new context—from the eyes of a mother—the difficulties Fatma and Mustafa must have experienced, their financial and physical hardships, and I recognized that maybe they had just wanted the best for me, as I did for John. But they had thought others could provide that for me better than they could, so they had given me away. I was blessed to be in different circumstances, where I could provide for my child. I had more choices available to me than they had had. I could decide what sort of parent I wanted to be.

It was progress. After that, I returned to Turkey regularly.

Chapter Sixteen

"If God had commanded me to do all things I could do them."
—1 Nephi 17:50

LONDON, ONTARIO, WAS A SMALL, pretty town surrounded by country fields, and it housed a good medical hospital and a renowned university. It was a small enough place that I could walk to wherever I needed to go, and I enjoyed walking along the aptly named Thames River that ran through town. Especially in the springtime, I would take John for walks in nature and feel blessed to have been given another spring. It was my favorite time of year, when the whole earth woke from a long sleep. I loved the scent of the tender leaves and flowers. The magnolia trees burst into blossom, like elegantly gowned women all dressed up but standing around with nowhere to go. The wind in the maple trees sounded like the ocean. I loved the sounds of the birds singing early in the morning and began to recognize the different birds by their voices. I wrote in my journal:

God has given us the most beautiful place to live. I hope we can keep it, preserve it, and pass it on to the next generation. Sometimes I worry about the fact that when our great-grandchildren inherit this earth, they will also inherit many problems too. However, we cannot give up hope for the best. We must have unshakable faith and move forward each and every day.

I enjoyed my Church membership in that town and grew strong roots in the gospel and made a lot of friends. These people had children John's age, and it was good to watch him learn to socialize and make friends of his own. I also met new friends through attending the university in

London. Our life there was stable, and it was a good place to raise a child. Even though Ross traveled a lot, I didn't feel alone because of the "family" I had at church.

Some of my professors continued to take me under their wings and teach me that instead of raising my voice, I should raise my education level, and then people would listen to me. That was great advice; education was a key that opened any door.

One of my greatest gains from the time we lived in London was the friendship I formed with Joanne McLeish. She was an incredible friend and support to me and remains so to this day. Through her, I learned there are many wonderful people in the world, all doing wonderful things, but most of them are silent heroes. They just go about quietly doing good in their day-to-day lives. Joanne was one of these. She inspired me to want to improve myself so that I, too, could be of help to those around me. I wanted to be a useful person.

With Ross away half the year, it was sometimes difficult to help John realize his father's absence was nothing to do with him, that it was Ross's job, and that he would rather be home with his son than leave him behind. Because of this, when possible, I homeschooled John so we could travel with Ross and John could spend time with him. It was not an easy task to homeschool him, but we managed. He became an adept little traveler. Other small children often have difficulty when their routines change or when they are expected to sleep in a strange new place, but John was very adaptable to new circumstances. I believed travel was a great education for him in itself. But we always had the family tradition that no matter where in the world we were, we would return home to London for Christmas. London always had lots of snow, and it was a beautiful place to spend the holidays together.

Through the years, Ross and I became avid world travelers. I always enjoyed going to new places and seeing new things, and thanks to Ross's job, we were in a position to go to many different countries in the world. In the United States alone, from Hawaii to Alaska, I visited forty states. We went to Belgium, Holland, France, Luxembourg, Turkey, Cuba, Germany, England, the Bahamas, the Caribbean, Thailand, Malaysia, and Japan, to name a few. It has never taken much to entice me; suggest a trip, and I'm ready to go at the drop of a hat. (During the collaboration on this book alone, I sometimes vexed Kristen by simply disappearing for weeks on end, once to Florida, twice to Utah, and twice to Turkey.)

Each country we visited brought a new perspective to our lives. The more I traveled, the more I recognized how alike people are. We truly are brothers and sisters. It doesn't matter where we are from; we each have similar joys and sorrows, trials and challenges. During our travels, we were privileged to attend sacrament meetings in different parts of the world. It didn't matter where we were; the gospel of Jesus Christ was the same.

A few of our adventures have stood out in my mind. Once in Thailand I saw a very wrinkly, very small old man crouched on the ground at the end of the market. He was facing the sun and eating an apple he was dipping into coconut from a little bag. He was enjoying that apple like there was nothing more beautiful in the world. I sat down a distance away and watched him, entranced, for quite some time. How could he be so happy over something so simple as an apple? His face was exuberant with joy. I had never seen anyone lit up quite that way before. Later I learned that apples don't grow in Thailand and are extremely rare there. However he had obtained this rare treat, he had certainly enjoyed it. That small incident gave me a new perspective and made me wonder what was missing in my life. I should enjoy my life every minute as much as he enjoyed that apple.

At a Buddhist temple in Thailand, I saw an elderly woman walking along with a bunch of small, ripe bananas. Curious, I watched as she approached the small pool by the temple, knelt, and lightly touched the still surface of the water with the palm of her hand, making small ripples. Immediately a bunch of turtles rushed over to her, responding to the signal, and she fed them bits of ripe banana. Touched, I thought to myself, *Look at this woman. She values all life so much. I should learn to value what is around me.* I sometimes don't see the little details. There are lessons to be learned in every small thing.

Once, on the way to Los Angeles, we drove through the Mojave Desert, and that was an experience by itself. Such heat in that barren land. The heat waves shimmered on the horizon, making the distant hills look like they were floating on water. I don't know how the cowboys survived, riding their horses day after day in that intense sun. Turkey is hot and dry, yes, and the brown rock of the Mojave reminded me somewhat of home, but in Istanbul there was always a breeze from the sea. The water was never far away. It was a completely different experience to drive through that endless desert oven. I found all that immensity very humbling, and it gave me a greater appreciation for the variety God created.

Not all of my adventures were happy ones. In Dubai I saw a woman commit suicide. I was at the beach, and the woman, a foreign tourist from some unknown place, walked out into the ocean . . . and kept on walking. Her dark head disappeared beneath the water, and it took me awhile to realize she wasn't intending to come back. Someone else saw too, and an ambulance and helicopter were summoned, but even though they retrieved the woman and brought her to shore, they were unable to revive her. I was stunned that someone could dislike themselves so much that they would keep walking into the water knowing they weren't coming back. It affected me a great deal. Even though I had been suicidal myself several times, it was somehow different, seeing it from the outside and seeing it from my new LDS perspective. My heart ached for this woman I didn't know and now never would know. And it made me grateful that I had never succeeded in my own suicide attempts. Think of all I would have missed.

In Japan I got the distinct impression that they did not like outsiders and felt they were well enough off without foreigners around. Ross and I took a city bus tour, and though it was meant for tourists to the country, it was conducted entirely in Japanese. I felt quite stupid.

Through my travels, I learned to see myself as a member of a great sisterhood of women across the world. I saw women living in all sorts of circumstances and in every conceivable condition, and I saw the amazing things they did with their lives. As I recognized the power and innate ability of women to meet the challenges of their lives and accomplish great things, I felt a stirring within me that I was to do some important work too, though I didn't know what.

* * *

Like the time Dad came to me in the dream at the time of his death, I've had promptings and knowledge given to me many times when I've needed it. Once we went to Niagara to go camping, but we had no sooner arrived and started to set up our tent than I had the strong impression we should hurry back home again. I sensed that Ross's mother was in trouble. I told

Ross, "Pack the car back up. We have to go home." Ross never questioned the promptings I received. We jumped back in the car and returned home to learn that Ross's mother had been admitted to the hospital.

Throughout the years, Mother Hitchins and I had come to love each other. As she was nearing death, she told me she was glad I had married her son and that I was the best wife Ross could have had. That meant so much to me and to Ross as well.

Ross was supposed to serve as best man at his friend Fred's upcoming wedding in Chicago (just as Fred had served as Ross's best man at our wedding). Ross's mother told him to go ahead and keep the commitment he had made to Fred, so we went, but on the way back to Canada, I felt a strong impression that we should not return home but should go straight to the hospital. I felt his mother was just holding on, waiting for Ross to arrive. Ross did get there just in time to be with her before she died.

It was sad for me to think that this kind woman was leaving us, and I felt a large part of me was being taken away. However, now I was armed with the knowledge the gospel had given me of life after death and the great plan of salvation, so her death was not the devastating event my father's death had been. This time I understood that I would see her again and that she was with the beloved husband she had lost so many years before.

* * *

On another occasion, the "sense" I felt would have a great impact on the course my life would take. One night when John was small, I dreamt that a gentleman from Salt Lake City came to see me about a project of some sort. I wasn't clear what the project was, but I felt it was something important. The only person I knew from Salt Lake was a friend named Brother Rasmussen, who was living in London. I told him about the dream. I told him I felt I was going to be involved in something serious, but I didn't know what it was. And I wasn't sure how this would be brought about in my already busy life.

Brother Rasmussen told me he was headed to Salt Lake to see the Brethren (I believe he was in the Church Educational System) and that he would mention the dream to them. I was startled that he had taken my story so seriously, and I wondered what I had gotten myself into. I was soon to find out.

When he returned from his trip, Brother Rasmussen came to see me.

"The Brethren told me they have been praying to find someone to do a Turkish translation of the Book of Mormon," he said.

I was floored. Was this what my premonition had been pointing to? Were they looking for *me*? That would be a much bigger and more important project than I had anticipated.

"They told me they haven't been able to find anyone yet," Brother Rasmussen explained. "I told them about you, and they are going to send you a translation test to take."

After he left, I sat and thought for a long time. My head and heart were filled with indescribable feelings. How many Church members were there who spoke Turkish? Was this perhaps what I was meant to do? Would I be capable of undertaking such a monumental endeavor? Would God trust me to do something like that? The staggering implication was that, if I *was* the one the Brethren were seeking to do this task, it meant God was aware of *me*.

Gradually, the bombardment of feeling distilled into an excited, warm anticipation. If this indeed was what my life had been leading up to, I was prepared to accept whatever the Lord wanted me to do, and I felt confident that He would somehow give me the ability to do it.

The test duly arrived, and I filled it out and returned it. I didn't know how I had done, but I felt I'd completed it to the best of my ability. I can tell you there was none of that former confidence and pride I'd felt after taking my university music ability test.

Then two people from Church headquarters came to see me. They told me they wanted me to serve on the small working group that would translate the Book of Mormon into Turkish. I would not have to work alone but would be part of a team, which I found greatly encouraging. While we were talking, they also mentioned they were looking for someone with a musical background who could translate some of the hymns for use by Turkish people living in Germany. This also struck me. What were the odds that they would be led to me, a Church member with knowledge of the Turkish language *and* training in music?

While things unfolded, Ross's employer suddenly decided to relocate him and gave him a choice of a few places, including Winnipeg, Manitoba. My stomach sunk a little with that option. All I knew about it was that it was cold there. We loved London and didn't want to go to Winnipeg, but after praying about it, we knew we should. So once again, life was in transition. Cihangir decided to come with us. We arrived in May and found it snowing. It was a shock, and it should have given us a clue of what to expect. I've never been as cold as during the time we lived in Winnipeg.

As it turned out, our two-year stay in Winnipeg was one of the highlights of our lives. Ross began his work at the Department of National Defence right away. Cihangir managed to find good employment. I tried my best to make our new house a home. I had to orient myself to a new place, find the local stores, find a new doctor, find a new dentist, enroll John in school, meet new neighbors, and find our new ward. We were welcomed with open arms the very first Sunday we attended St. James ward, especially by the Diaczun family. Since the day we met, we have become inseparable.

It seems to be a pattern in my life that, lacking a strong birth family, I create my own family wherever I go. First, Pakize Ercan and her children, then the Poultons, and now the Diaczuns, among others. They've all become more than friends to me; they have become family. The Diaczuns' daughter Mallory was John's age, and she instantly became John's playmate. Their son Craig was much older than John, but it didn't take long before John was following him around like a puppy. Their other daughters, Holly and Jill, completed John's new circle of friendship.

Their acceptance made the move so much easier for us. I firmly believe God arranged for our path to cross with the Diaczuns' at just the moment when we most needed them. Ross was called as the first counselor, while Steven Diaczun served as bishop, and I was called as the Primary president, with Penny Diaczun as my counselor. Serving together side by side strengthened our friendship. What a blessing it was to see our children grow together. It was never easy to start over on short notice in a new city, but thanks to the love and support of the Diaczuns, we never felt alone in Winnipeg. They were our sunshine in "Friendly Manitoba." Through them, I learned the importance of befriending strangers and welcoming those who are new with open hands and an open heart. It can be life-changing for both parties involved. I think sometimes we underestimate the importance a friend can play in a person's life, especially if the timing and the need are positioned just right. At the time, I wrote in my journal:

The gospel of Jesus Christ changes our lives forever. Each unique life touches another, and once we are touched, we are never the same.

During my Winnipeg years, my involvement in the translation project and my responsibilities as a mother did not leave me with much free time, but I continued to pursue my education in Winnipeg just as I had in London. Since I could not attend day classes, I took several night classes at the University of Winnipeg when Ross was home to watch John. The winter nights were extremely cold, and it could dip to negative twenty-five or thirty degrees Celsius (which would be negative twenty-two degrees Fahrenheit). The university was downtown, and I rode the bus. There were days I had to touch my nose to feel if it was still attached to my frozen face. While I had experienced dry cold in Turkey, it was not like this bone-deep, eyeball-searing cold. And it didn't seem to matter how many layers of clothing I put on. It would take me fifteen minutes to put on all my winter gear, covering everything but my eyes, and I would still feel numb when I walked outside. My breath would soak my scarf, and it would freeze stiff. My boots made the snow squeak underfoot. The snow would be piled head-high at the side of the streets so it was like walking down a gray-white tunnel. Going to school under such circumstances was no easy task, but then again, nothing I have achieved in my life has come to me easily.

With determination and perseverance as weeks rolled into months, we took up our new lives in this new place. I could feel my testimony of the gospel growing stronger and stronger. I could feel the presence of the Lord in my everyday life. Often I found myself on my knees, praying for guidance and direction. I felt there was so much to celebrate and enjoy in life.

It was during this time, as I said, that I was immersed in work on the translation project.

* * *

Before beginning the monumental task of the Book of Mormon translation, I was instructed to translate a selection of twenty hymns into Turkish. The Brethren indicated which hymns I was to focus on. I found it an interesting challenge to make the translation accurate but still fit it to the musical score. Before every translation session, I learned to pray for assistance in finding the right words. During the translation, I developed the habit of praying to know that I was accurately capturing the message and feeling of the hymn, and after I finished, I prayed again in gratitude that I had completed the task and to thank Heavenly Father for His guidance. If I missed these steps, the translation did not go well. Through trial and error, I learned not to rely on myself alone but to rely on the guidance of the Spirit. This was no longer just a theoretical or intellectual understanding; I learned to depend on the Spirit as a tangible, working force in my life.

Incidentally, I never saw the finished hymnbook I helped compile in 1990 until we picked up John from his mission to Utah in 2008. It was in a bookstore in Provo that I first saw the Turkish hymnbook. There it was on the shelf. I couldn't help it; I started crying. Of course, I bought one to take home.

The Book of Mormon project started in 1991 and took about eight years to complete. It was indeed a team effort. The members of the translation committee lived in various places across the world but had to work closely together, which was a challenge in those days before the Internet and e-mail were available. Today it would be possible to consult with each other constantly online or through webcasts and video conferencing, but back then, the logistics alone were rather daunting, and the phone bills were staggering. Fortunately the Church paid for all but postage.

The director of the project was a linguist named Chris DeSantis, who lived in Salt Lake City. The chief translator was Murat Cakir, also in Salt Lake. A non-LDS woman in Istanbul, whose name I unfortunately do not recall, was a specialist in grammar and checked the technicalities of the language. My job was to take Murat's translation and review the content to make sure the doctrine was correct. The work required a lot of back-and-forth exchanges because the changes one person made might impact the work of another. If I reviewed a passage to make sure the content was correct and then sent it to the woman in Istanbul, her corrections to the grammar might potentially alter the meaning of the content, so it would have to come back to me so I could double-check it.

It was humbling to do this work. As with the hymn translation, we would pray before working, and sometimes we had prayer together by three-way phone calls. I spent many hours deep in study and conversation, making sure I had a thorough understanding of the concepts and doctrine so I could catch any errors. As someone who had been in the Church fewer than ten years, I knew my own limitations, and it seemed the more

I learned, the more I realized I didn't know. One precept would lead into another, and whole worlds were opened to my view so that I would find myself saying, "Look at that. See how these are connected," and that would lead me yet further. The principles of the gospel were glorious to me, and that period of time greatly enriched my testimony.

Also during this time, I felt it especially crucial that I live my life according to the precepts of the gospel—the best possible life I could live—so I was ready and able to receive inspiration and personal revelation. I knew it was important for me to keep myself clean and worthy and keep my life in line with the principles I knew to be true so God could work with me as a tool in His hand. If I had a rough day or had a fight with Ross, if I was impatient with Cihangir or felt sleep-deprived, I struggled to regain the Spirit and return to a good place so I was in the correct frame of mind to do the work. It was not something I could force.

I once recorded in my journal:

I have a strong testimony of God and of His strong presence in my life. He has never forsaken me. He always listens to my soul's complaints. Although I don't always understand everything, I know He does. He knows what is in my heart. He knows my needs and my heart's desires. I have a unique relationship with my Savior too. He loves me and carries me in time of need. I am in need of His constant care in my daily life. It is a wonderful feeling to have someone in my life who loves me for who I am and not what I am. Even when I fall short, He makes up the difference. I am grateful for His Atonement. I will never fully understand the meaning of the Atonement, but I do know it was meant for me as well as anybody else. I hope to endure to the end so He can say: "Well done, my faithful servant!"

As I worked, the thought often came to me that I was helping to lay a foundation for my people back in Turkey and that the Book of Mormon translated into their language would be a key to freeing them and bringing them into the light of the gospel. I gained an awareness of how much I cared about the Turkish people as a whole, and my friends and acquaintances in particular. I wondered if this was what my life had been meant for, to bring me to this very point and enable me to help them in whatever role I could. I began to explore this new purpose and my growing desire to be of help to others.

Many beautiful and sacred experiences came out of my work with the translation team. I was blessed with perceptions and visions of events so I would know how to translate them. I was blessed with an understanding of the doctrine of the Church far beyond my personal abilities. I strongly felt I was an instrument in the Lord's hands.

Once all four of us on the translation committee met in Istanbul, partly to decide how to translate the name of the Church. It was a difficult matter because we wanted to highlight Christ in the name (and similarly, the Church later officially changed its logo to make Christ's name central to and larger than the rest of the words). We felt it was important to have the name reflect exactly what heaven intended.

Throughout the course of the years, we had to start over on the translation of the Book of Mormon three times in order to get it right. We found after reaching a certain point that the personality of the translator started to intrude, and we did not want it to influence the work. We didn't want our word selection or the cadence of the language to be colored by *our* thoughts or personalities. We wanted the spirit of the book to come through untainted by our hands. We were all perfectly in accord with each other with regard to this intention. So we would start again. Far from being discouraged by this, I felt invigorated. Heavenly Father was truly guiding the work and making sure it came out how He wanted, and He would work with us, faulty though we might be, to bring about His purposes.

Chapter Seventeen

"Even if ye can no more than desire to believe,
let this desire work in you."
—*Alma 32:27*

I HAVE LEARNED IN MY life not to cling too tightly to any set of individual circumstances. Happy as we may be with one situation, life always has a new path or a new beginning to present, and we have to be open to whatever the universe offers in order not to miss out on the blessings that can come with it. I have heard it said that if you cling to anything too tightly, your hands are in fists and then they are not open and able to receive whatever gift life wants to give you next. It has been a lifelong challenge for me to learn to open my hands.

After two pleasant and happy years in Winnipeg, it came time to leave. I was very sorry to let this new place and my new friends go, but it was time to return to London, a place where I had also been happy. We still had our house there and returned to live in it for nearly twelve years more. That was the longest I have ever lived in one spot in my life, and I was content there. I felt quite at home. It was a lesson to me; I had been reluctant to leave London, and then I was reluctant to leave Winnipeg, but I found I could be happy in either—or *any*—place. Home was wherever Ross and John were.

Cihangir didn't return to Ontario with us immediately but remained working in Manitoba. I worried about him because his life did not seem to run any more smoothly for him than it had for me at that age. Some of that was brought about by his choices. He was heavily into drugs and alcohol and eventually lost his good job. He rejoined us in London, but after he had been in Canada a total of thirteen years, the government deported him to Turkey. I was very sorry about this and worried about what would happen to him. I told myself that Ross and I had done all we could for him, that Cihangir needed to face the consequences of his own choices, but I was still upset about his deportation and felt in a small way that I had failed my brother. I loved him deeply and wanted things to turn out well for him. The things we suffered together as children had strengthened the love between us, creating a bond that could not be broken.

Fortunately, Cihangir took his deportation as a wake-up call and realized he needed to do something with his life. He eventually made a good life for himself in Istanbul, married, and found good employment as a businessman. I am proud of him and how he has turned his circumstances around. It has been a hard climb for him, but he has persevered and succeeded.

* * *

It was in London when John was three or four that I really began to take joy in being a mother. Gradually, I realized I was going to be okay as a mom. After that, I relaxed, and life was good. I read and researched and developed new skills in parenting. I was usually a joyful person by nature, but being with John gave me a deep, abiding happiness that no other experience could match. Whenever he needed me to play or talk with him, I would drop everything to spend time with my little boy.

My father had read to me all my childhood, and it was a joy to me to read with John the same stories I had shared with my dad. It felt as if I was connecting the generations, and it was healing for me. I could imagine Dad there with us, see his smile, picture him enjoying this beautiful little boy's company. Our favorite stories were Beatrix Potter's tales, and we collected the series in several different editions, all sizes and kinds. John especially liked those. I read the scriptures with him as well and sang Primary songs with him. I had, of course, missed out on Primary myself, and I was glad my child could participate in that lovely program.

John was a happy child, but he could be stubborn. I would take him grocery shopping with me, and at the store there was a little box where you could take a candy. A sign told you to please deposit ten cents in return. Sometimes I let John put in a dime and take a candy. Once when he was about four years old, an elderly friend accompanied us to the store. John watched her take a candy from the box and eat it, but she didn't deposit the ten cents. John, riding in the cart, muttered, "That old woman didn't put ten cents in the box. She's eating the candy."

I didn't want to hurt my friend's feelings, so I said nothing. But as we continued around the store, John kept repeating the accusation, getting louder and louder and more and more red in the face. Finally I hissed at him, "Back off. It's okay."

"It's not okay," he cried shrilly at the top of his lungs. "She ate the candy and didn't put in her ten cents."

Finally my elderly friend said, "Enough is enough. I'm putting in the ten cents, okay? There. Now just shut up."

When John knew something was right or wrong, he wouldn't be budged from it. He understood justice and never hesitated to point out anything that was unfair.

It was a joy to me to watch my son as he grew in the gospel and was baptized—by Ross, just as I had once hoped—and received the priesthood. Ross and I could see in John the inherent goodness he had brought with him into this life, the gifts God had blessed him with, and we did our best to nurture and magnify that goodness. I made it my mission to always be there for John. One of my biggest accomplishments is to be able to say that whenever he did something, I was there to see it. Whatever John did, I did it too. When he joined Cub Scouts, I became a Cub leader. When he went into scuba diving, I took lessons with him . . . though neither of us ended up ready to go into the ocean. It was too scary.

John never did get over his stubbornness though. Years after the candy incident, he was working on his Duty to God Award, which included the challenge of reading the Book of Mormon. He got very close to completing it but grew tired of the effort and wanted to quit. I would read to him sometimes to help him through it. He finally decided he did not want to finish the book. When I announced, "I'm going to read!" he would go to his room, close the door, and sit with his back to it, refusing to participate or let me in. I didn't let this deter me; I could be just as stubborn as he. I would sit outside his room in the hallway and read aloud. He would call to me to stop, and I'd call back, "The hallway is public space," and keep reading. We finished the

Book of Mormon at last, he got his medal (the first in our stake to do so), and later he thanked me for getting him through.

Like any boy, sometimes John wouldn't want to go to school. I told him the only way he could get out of going to school was if he was dead and that even then I would toss his body in the car and drive him around the school. He asked, "What about my agency?" and I replied (jokingly, of course), "Your agency doesn't kick in until you are twenty-five. Until then, your parents will make your decisions for you." (I'm pleased to report that John has consistently made very good decisions all his life.)

John inherited my love of argument as well. Sometimes we got into fierce verbal battles. Once Ross tried to intervene and told us to calm down. John stopped, looked at Ross, and said calmly, "It's okay, Dad. We love each other. It's just the way we speak to each other."

I continued my schooling, and it took me nine years to finish a four-year degree. I wanted to tell my son someday, when it was his turn to go to a university, that I wasn't asking him to do anything I hadn't done myself. I wanted to set a good example and show him how much I valued education. I never told him to do anything or live by any principle unless I had also done it myself. Growing up, John often told Ross, "Mom knows what she's talking about. She means what she says."

* * *

In about 1999, on one of my trips back to Karaman, I learned that Omer was very ill. I was troubled by this news and went to see him. He was about fifty by then but looked much older. I was shocked by his appearance. He had kidney failure, and I took him to the hospital at one point for a blood transfusion because he was extremely pale. But the physician told me there was no point in giving it to him, that it wouldn't help him. It was too late for anything to be done. Shortly before Omer died, I visited him at the hospital, and he begged me to "put him to sleep" with poison. Of course, I couldn't think of that, but it was difficult to watch him suffer, knowing that much of it he had brought upon himself. Even though I knew he wasn't truly my older brother, I still thought of him that way. In spite of the turmoil he had caused my parents and the disruption he had brought to my already unstable childhood, I felt great compassion for him and wished his ending could have been otherwise. The gospel once again helped me cope with his death and keep a perspective that the rest of my family could not.

* * *

At about the same time Omer died, the translation project of the Book of Mormon came to an end. When it was finally finished, the enormity of the task really sank into me as I felt the joyful burden of the responsibility lift from me. I had served God in a focused way for eight years. I had been a tool in His hands, which had been a great privilege and honor, and there was both a sense of accomplishment and gratitude and a sense of loss when it was over. I knew I wanted to keep that depth of understanding I had attained. I wanted to preserve the study habits I had incorporated into the last eight years. I felt somewhat at loose ends. I imagine it was much the same as a missionary feels, returning home to a regular life after two years of unwavering focus and dedication, knowing that life will likely never again reach that kind of intensity. When I was presented with the final printed copy of the Turkish Book of Mormon, I wept and wept.

* * *

London was good for us, but life still had more to offer, and we eventually accepted a move to Mississauga, a busy city of seven hundred thousand people two and a half hours from London. After our being so long in one place, moving to our new home in Mississauga was not easy for our family, especially for John, who was a teenager and had to cope with leaving friends and switching schools. I didn't know what lay before us in this new place . . . but I took this on as yet another good challenge.

One of the biggest problems we faced was living in a hotel for more than three months. While Ross was travelling in China on business, John and I lived in the Marriott Residency. It didn't matter how many stars that hotel might have had, living in such a setting with a broad-shouldered teenager was challenging. There was never enough space or light or food or active entertainment. The Diaczun family, who had also moved from Winnipeg to Mississauga by this time, came to our rescue many times. Their home became our home, and we were a family once again. We shared more than just meals. They became my strength during those challenging times. Our friendship stood the test of time, and I feel it is safe to say our love and family ties can only be measured in an eternal realm. When Steven and Ross were both called to serve as counselors together in the Mississauga stake, we knew with surety once more that the Lord was touching our lives in a very wonderful way. I have drawn great strength from that friendship.

On March 17, 2003, we officially moved in to our new place. This time it did not take me long to turn our new house into a home. I wanted my new place to reflect all that I loved and valued. Today it is a place of warmth and welcome, of friends and family. My doors and windows are open; it is a space of light and music and growing things, and I have placed reminders of Turkey throughout the house—colorful rugs, carved wooden furniture, and bright fabrics. These things cheer me and remind me of all I have done, all I have been, and all the things that matter to me.

One advantage to living in Mississauga was that the Toronto temple was now only half an hour away. I arranged to attend as often as I could. Going to the temple made me feel complete, and I found it a great place to look for answers. Whether they were big or small, God always granted my wishes as long as they were righteous and pleasing to Him.

Just as we were getting into our new routine, I decided to look for work. John was in high school by this time, and I felt he was able to manage his life more independently. I was in a position to utilize my education and support our household income. And I also had a desire to use what I had learned through training or experience to help other people in a tangible way. So I began to search for work.

I had never found full-time work before. All my other jobs had been part-time and sometimes just volunteer positions, not paying employment. I soon discovered that finding employment having to do with sociology was impossible in my area of the city. I was trained as a family mediator, and because my field was highly specialized, I could only work at certain kinds of places. One of these places happened to be family court.

After much research and prayer, I was able to find employment, but my new workplace was ninety-five kilometers (fifty-eight miles) away from home in a town called Oshawa on the shores of Lake Ontario. This meant that I was going to drive almost two hundred kilometers (one hundred twenty-four miles) a day to work and back. Like any other challenge in my life, I welcomed this one as an opportunity for growth. It is hard to believe that eight years have now passed since my humble beginnings at the Superior Court in Oshawa.

Sometimes I smile when people ask me why I drive one thousand kilometers a week on insanely busy freeways for such little income. I guess I do it because I love helping people. People are my passion. When people come to my office with their stress, worries, and every other roller coaster of emotion in between, I look deep into their souls and try to understand their sorrow. At one time or another, life can be challenging for all of us. Having gone through so much difficulty in life myself, I can empathize with their situations. I know what it is to face a difficulty that seems insurmountable, to feel alone, to doubt your own abilities, and to have to summon incredible internal strength. I understand loss and depression from an insider's point of view, and I think the people I work with in family court can sense that my empathy is real.

As a mediator with the court, I am intimately involved in the struggles and challenges of families. In a family breakup, there are no winners. Breakups can cause deep scars in the human soul. My job is to offer alternatives. I try to teach people the principle of never running out of options. There's always something more to try. I am truly grateful I am in a position to move people forward if they choose to do so. Being stuck can be a lonely place.

I have a soft spot in my heart for young parents. I know how easy it is to become overwhelmed and burdened, to doubt yourself and your abilities. I try to work especially diligently with young couples. I firmly believe that it is never too late to learn new ways of living. I love helping people help themselves. It is a lesson I have practiced over and over again throughout my life.

I once wrote in my journal:

As a family, we are blessed beyond measure. We could not ask for a better life! God must really love us. I am happy to be working in Oshawa, earning good money for something I love doing. I love helping people. I love people! . . . I have the best job in the world. How many people can say they absolutely love their job and look forward to going to work every day? I am truly blessed beyond measure! I have a wonderful family and wonderful job. What a priceless combination!

Chapter Eighteen

"And now behold, I say unto you, my brethren, if ye have experienced a change of heart, and if ye have felt to sing the song of redeeming love, I would ask, can ye feel so now?"
—Alma 5:26

SINCE JOINING THE CHURCH I have always done my best to keep the commandments and the commitments I have made. But I always struggled with the commandment to honor one's parents. That one point was particularly difficult for me. How could I honor Turkan, the woman I had thought was my mother, when she had behaved in such an abusive way toward me? How could I honor Fatma and Mustafa, who had given me away? There were times in my life that I felt I was never going to forgive my parents. I felt they deserved to suffer just as much as I had. After all, I had not asked for all the sorrow and pain. Since I did not have much by way of worldly goods, the only things I could withhold from them were my love and respect. After I joined the Church and came to know this particular commandment, it was not easy for me to observe it, though I wanted to do it. I spent a lot of time in prayer before God, searching for a way to live this commandment, praying for a softer, more forgiving heart.

I had learned that God could open a way when to me there seemed to be no way, and that truth manifested itself again in this case. One day in sacrament meeting, I learned a different meaning to honoring one's father and mother. The speaker explained that it could also mean living in such a way that your parents could be proud of you, bringing honor to the family name. That, I felt, I could do. I could bring them honor through the life I lived.

Where once the concept of family was a challenge for me, it eventually became everything to me. I once wrote to Church headquarters asking for permission to be sealed to my father, Necmi Gencata. I didn't receive an answer to my query, but some time later I received a letter telling me his temple work had been done. Someone in Salt Lake City had done it, and it was a total surprise to me. I confess I felt a little taken aback; I had expected that Ross would be his proxy in the temple, but it was not to be. I told myself it didn't matter as long as the temple work had been done. But I was troubled at the thought of not being sealed to the wonderful man who had raised me. I couldn't imagine a heaven where I wasn't with him. I finally went to see my bishop to talk about it. I wasn't sure what to do.

"Sister Hitchins," my bishop said, "I would advise you to wait and think about it for a long time. In the meantime, you need to be working on your forgiveness, especially toward your biological parents."

It wasn't what I wanted to hear. Did God really expect me to forgive Fatma and Mustafa? I felt like telling God, "Look at all the progress I've made. Isn't that enough?" Surely this was asking too much. But the bishop was right, of course. Things were still tense between my birth parents and me, and that wasn't the way God wanted it to be in a family. And they *were* family, after all. The bishop's counsel proved its worth over the years as I slowly started thinking differently about my biological parents. It was necessary for me to learn about them and understand them and the position they had been in before I could really forgive and love them. It wasn't my role to judge or change them. With that understanding came peace.

After many heartfelt discussions, I truly began to understand my birth parents' place in life. Life had not been kind to them. My mother, Fatma, was fifteen years old when she was told she was to marry Mustafa, who was eleven years her senior. By that time, Mustafa was already divorced from his former wife because she could not have any children. Fatma must have been very scared at the thought of getting married at such a young age. She told me she used to hide in the hope chest when my father was mad at her. Poverty, lack of education, harsh living conditions, the constant pressure of the unwritten laws of tradition and culture, and many other oppressive forces had created an inescapable life for Fatma. There was no way out for either of my birth parents.

They were living from one day to the next, not knowing what tomorrow was going to bring. Fatma once told me she had felt trapped and helpless. Eleven months after giving birth to my brother Mehmet, she gave birth to me. Regardless of her health, she had to go back to work; she had no other choice. According to her, I was a very small, quiet child. She had no milk to feed me, so she fed me with boiled potatoes and molasses every night. Two years later she had my brother Mustafa. I can't imagine how difficult it must have been for her, practically a child herself, to have three children by the time she was nineteen years old.

My father, Mustafa, was gone for days. He was the village ranger, with very little pay. Sometimes he was gone for weeks at a time, leaving my mother all alone. She had no help from anyone. In that patriarchal society, she had no right to question her husband's whereabouts. He was the man of the house, and that was that; he was not obligated to explain anything to anyone. When his older sister, Turkan, came to ask him for one of their children, he did not have a long discussion with my mother. In fact, it was culturally expected in a rural community to honor the wishes of an older person. At the time of Turkan's visit forty-something years ago, things were very different from what they are today.

Turkan was very persuasive in her request to adopt me. All she wanted was to have a daughter, and she was going to give me a better life. After all, what kind of a life was waiting for me in this village? She had education, she had money, and she had a very supportive husband who was also in love with the idea of having a child. The only obstacle to their joint effort was Fatma.

She told me many times that she had been totally opposed to the idea of giving me up. She cried for hours to change her husband's mind. She felt he was making a big mistake by separating the siblings. I was her child, and she was my mother. I can see her mournful face in my mind's eye as she stood at the doorway of our mud home, saying good-bye to me. My father told her that they were young and they could always have other children in the future. Who would have known this tragic scene was to be repeated with Cihangir within a few years?

With every passing year, I got to know my biological parents a little better. When I first listened to Fatma's story, I was angry with Mustafa. However, I also knew the story had two sides. Mustafa admitted to me that he had been young and did not often think much about the consequences of his choices. All he wanted was to be respectful of his elder sister. After all, she was the one with education and money. Compared to her, he was nothing. She must have known what was best. He hadn't known about Turkan's mental illness then. If she was saying she was going to love me as her own daughter, I was only too lucky to have her as my mother. Back in those days, Istanbul was light-years away from my little, miserable village. All the good things in life were going to be at my disposal: good food, good clothes, good education, and a good mother. Who could ask for more than that? Who was he to say no to all this goodness? Who was Fatma to stand in the way of my happy life in Istanbul? What did she know, anyway? He firmly believed I was better off living in luxury than being lost in dusty Cukurbag. Whatever he did, he did it for me. He never said it in so many words, but I came to understand that he loved me so much he had to let me go. In his mind, it was a fair trade.

Now that I have raised my own child for twenty-three years, I understand my parents' feelings of wanting a better life for me. John's birth mother gave him up so he could have a better life. I am ever grateful she made perhaps the most difficult decision of her life when she placed him for adoption. It must have been extremely hard for her to say good-bye to her only child when he was only a few days old. The moment I saw my son, my heart melted. I knew for sure he was going to be my son forever. Did Turkan feel the same way when she first saw me? Did she know in her heart that I was going to be her only daughter forever? Did Fatma yearn for me to come back and be her daughter once again? Did Mustafa realize his miscalculations? I don't know all the answers, but I do understand things a little better now and am able to make peace with them.

My son has not found his biological mother yet. As difficult as it may be, I would like him to reunite with his biological mother, and I am sure when he feels ready, he will find her. For the record, he will always be my son, and I will always be his mother forever and ever. Sometimes my friends ask me if it feels different to love an adopted child because I did not give birth to him. Of course, I have nothing to compare it to. All I know is that I love John more than life itself, and if I knew giving my life would extend his, I would gladly give mine up. His father and I made a covenant to love him, respect him, honor him, and raise him righteously because he is our greatest gift from Heavenly Father.

When we picked John up from his mission in 2008, we attended a testimony meeting the night before he was to leave. Many of John's former companions who had already gone home returned to hear him bear his last testimony as a missionary. Two of them sought us out afterward and told us what a great missionary John was. When Ross thanked them, they both said with passion, "No, you don't understand. We mean he was a *great* missionary." John had obviously touched their lives. I was so proud of him. I could not ask for a better son.

Time heals many wounds. There was a time when I couldn't stand being in Karaman, and strangely enough, now my heart arrives before the bus. I enjoy going back to Turkey to visit my parents and siblings. I love it when my whole family gathers around at dinnertime because there is so much laughter and joy as we reminisce about the old days, especially funny stories about Grandmother Havva. We finally learned to share our joy, as well as our sorrows. We are still in the process of getting to know one another. They don't ever have to worry about me anymore. I have kept my promise to my dad and feel I have become the daughter he always knew I would one day become.

Though I didn't tell my parents I had been baptized a Christian at first, little by little I have tried to extend Christlike kindness to them, and over the years, they have become reconciled to my new life. I have heard them defend my religious choices to others and even defend the Church itself. That is indeed a miracle.

While my relationship with my parents has healed a great deal, things are not quite as smooth with my brothers. I am trying to have a good relationship with Mustafa, and we are taking it one day at a time. But my relationship with Mehmet has never really healed, and we rarely talk. He has become an alcoholic and remains on the periphery of things. No one in the family really connects with him.

My younger sister, Hatice, has endured many challenges of her own. She quit school after sixth grade and ran away with a married man when she was fifteen. She had a daughter named Derya, whom she left with Fatma to raise when she was small, and went to Holland to work without legal status in that country. She simply showed up as a visitor and didn't go back. There she met another fellow and had a second child, a son named Yunus. This child she also left with Fatma for a number of years. For her part, Fatma wanted to raise these children in an effort to become a better mother to them than she felt she had been to Hatice. Having given away a son and daughter of her own, she was given another chance with another son and daughter to raise for a while. I suppose it has become something of a tradition in my family to raise other people's children.

Thanks to Ross's diligence and hard work, I have not had to worry about finances. He has been a great provider from the beginning, and I've always known we would have enough. That is so different from how I grew up, not knowing where the next piece of bread would come from. Like my father, I feel no need to have a lot of worldly goods, and I have found great joy in being able to share what I have with others. I bought Hatice a house and paid her a monthly salary so she could afford to stay home and not have to work for the last part of her children's growing-up years. I thought it was very important that she do this and believed it strengthened her own family in important ways. She and I have become friends more than sisters. When I go home, we gather around the woodstove and sip *sahlep* and enjoy the time we can spend together. We keep in touch through the Internet and wish we didn't live so far from each other. I am grateful for the miracle of modern technology that allows us to keep in touch over great distances.

My biological parents have been married now for fifty-two years. I often take care of them financially and pay for their needs too. I don't say any of this to boast but to show how the gospel has changed me. I have come a long way from the angry, resentful person I was. I am no longer the furious child trying to run away from Karaman. I have learned to let go of anger, to love and forgive.

* * *

I have discovered as I have grown older that I increasingly miss my country and the people there. Even though I have settled into my adopted country, somehow I feel just a little out of step in Canada; some small part of me is not in rhythm. I miss my land, my language, my family, and my friends. I long for the colors and smells and tastes and sounds of Turkey. I ordered Turkish television channels so I can hear my language, and I watch the Turkish news at night. I try to arrange to fly back at least once a year, though the brief visits don't seem to be enough to satisfy me. On one trip home a few years ago, I wrote in my journal:

There is so much history in Turkey. There is so much culture, beauty, and excitement. One does not look for life; life simply finds you. Every day is full of sound and color. People look after each other. People live together, die together, celebrate life together. . . . I miss this unique way of life. Maybe I am too nostalgic. . . . For now, I am going to enjoy every minute in Turkey. I am going to laugh, talk, share, and thank God for every little blessing in my life. Life is wonderful. God has granted us nothing but blessings, and I am eternally grateful for that.

Often my father's words to me that day in Karaman return to tease me: "If one day your life takes you back to Istanbul or even farther, Ayse, a part of you will still be here, whether you like it or not. You can't get away from who you are." Now it makes me smile to remember him saying that.

Other immigrants I know warned me that this longing for my homeland would eventually come, but I didn't give it much credence at the time. But the older I get, the more I understand what they and my father were trying to tell me. I certainly don't feel a desire to return to my childhood. But there is a sense of being too far from my roots, too far from who I really am deep inside. I am content with my life in Canada, but I also feel I could have a wonderful life back in Turkey.

Ross and John have accompanied me to Turkey several times. Throughout the years, Ross has grown to love the country, and he has always supported my efforts to maintain my culture and traditions (and he has survived all these years of my spicy cooking). I sometimes wondered if Ross could one day learn to see Turkey through my eyes and love that land enough that he would consider moving back there. Now I know the answer to that: we have purchased a little farmhouse in Karaman and plan to retire there shortly. More than anything, I would like to be a teacher in the little local school, teaching English, Turkish, history, and anything else the children are willing to learn.

My close friends keep telling me I am crazy, and perhaps I am. But I can hardly wait to go. I want to become one with the earth as I till the land. I want to plant many fruit trees in the yard and share the fruit with my neighbors. I want to gather fresh, warm eggs first thing in the morning and watch the fields explode with poppies in the spring. I want to smell the animals as they return from the pasture and watch the newborn goats as they jump around in the sunshine. Am I a dreamer? You bet. I hope I will continue to dream as I have done all my life, and I am happy to say that most of my dreams are now my reality.

* * *

In spite of all the healing I've undergone with regard to my family, I knew there was a final step I needed to take in order to have complete peace in my heart. I couldn't say I had truly followed my bishop's advice until I had confronted my feelings about Turkan, that dark shadow that still hovered behind everything.

Turkan had been living in the cave in Cukurbag since 1982 or 1983, and her health was very poor. After much argument with her, I returned to Turkey in 2007, took her from the cave, and brought her to my sister's house in Karaman, where Hatice took care of her. I paid for Mother's care, and little by little I began to look on her differently. I was no longer a hurt teenager rejecting those who had disappointed me. Now I was an adult with a child of my own. Slowly I began to see Mother for who she was, without viewing her through the filter of years of resentment and fear. I spent many long hours talking with her. I had consciously begun the process of trying to forgive her after my father died and especially after we adopted John, but it took many years to reach the point where I could feel not only comfortable but happy sitting with her and holding her hand as we talked.

"Ayse, are you here? Come and sit on the bed. I would like to talk to you," she once said.

"Yes, Mother, I am here. Don't worry. I am not going anywhere yet."

Sitting on her bed was a privilege since she did not want anyone else to come near her.

"You look tired today, Ayse. Did you sleep well?" she asked.

I thought it was nice of her to notice.

"I went to bed late, but I had enough sleep, Mother. Don't worry, I will be fine."

"My days are numbered," she said. "I feel the breath of death around me. It won't be long before I meet my Maker."

I was able to tell her honestly, "I love you, Mom." I paused, thinking about it, and then added sincerely, "I have always loved you."

"I love you too, Ayse. You have always been good to me, and I thank you for that." She told me she just wanted to pass away in her sleep without being a burden to anyone.

"You are not a burden, Mom. You are my mother, and I will always take care of you," I promised.

"Would you please give me my bath today?" she asked. "Wash my hair with your shampoo and don't forget to rinse it with your special cream. I don't like frizzy hair."

That made me smile. Even in her fragile condition, she wanted to look nice. *Good for her,* I thought. *Hopefully I will be just as full of life when I am eighty-two.*

"Sure, Mom," I answered. "I will wash you and make sure your hair is beautiful."

She looked so thin, only skin and bones. Once a mighty woman, ruler of my world, controller of my universe, she was now simply a small, fragile, elderly lady. I was able to look at her with love instead of fear or longing. As she held my hand, I felt her warmth. Maybe for the first time in my life, I was truly beginning to understand that she was also a child of God. Her Creator loved her just as much as He loved me.

As I began to wash her old body with warm water, I watched her face. She looked happy. It was great to see her happy. To my surprise, my heart did not ache anymore. I wanted to see her happy. With every drop of water, my soul was also being cleansed of all the toxic feelings I had harbored all those years. In that moment, I knew with surety that in spite of everything, in spite of our difficult history, she would always be my mother, and only God could judge her. Letting go of my ill feelings set my soul free. I was not her judge anymore, only her little daughter. I could serve her in this small way.

After her bath, I dried her silvery white hair. As she looked in the mirror, she was pleased to see that her hair was not frizzy.

"You look beautiful, Mom."

"You should have seen me when I was young. Your father fell in love with me because of my beauty."

I am sure that was very true. I had seen her photos.

"You are still beautiful, Mom. Look at you."

She came near the mirror to examine her face more closely. I stood right next to her. At that moment, I felt that our picture of happiness was complete. We both loved what we saw in the mirror. Mother and daughter, side by side, smiling. Nothing else mattered; there was no bitter history—only us. Once again, I had learned to open my fists and let go. It was such a light, freeing, and joyful feeling.

It was very difficult to say good-bye. I wished I could stay in Karaman and look after her myself, but I had to go back to Canada. Although my sister promised to look after her, I knew for sure she would not be able to keep her promise for long. My mother was not the easiest person in the world to live with. Her mental health was not stable, and her physical care was becoming demanding too.

As it turned out, I was right about my sister; she could not handle my mother. She tried but just couldn't manage that level of care. Turkan began to have bad dreams, and the nightmares made her scream in the middle of the night. The neighbors began complaining. They didn't know her condition, and we couldn't explain her challenges, so eventually my sister had to move Mom to Mustafa's home in Karaman.

Turkan didn't like being in her half brother's home, but I must admit that Mustafa went above and beyond the call of duty to take good care of her, and at the time, he was seventy-eight years old himself. Turkan slept all day and stayed up all night because she was afraid of dying; someone had once told her that most deaths happen in the dark hours of the night. At one point we placed her in a nursing home, but a short time later, the director of the nursing home called and demanded that we take her out of there. She was driving the staff and other patients crazy, and she had begun a hunger strike. Turkan was glad to leave because she never liked that place. She always presented herself like the Lady of Istanbul, with polished language and an elegant and dignified manner. That had never changed, even when she was carting her slop bucket from the cave for all those years.

Toward the end of her life, Turkan began to starve herself in order to hasten her death. She was very unhappy and just wanted to go. We had many long talks together on the phone. She told me she loved me and asked if I thought Dad would forgive her. Of course, I couldn't know for certain, but I knew my father's gentle heart and compassionate spirit. I remembered how he had taught me that caring for another person was an honor. So I smiled and said, "I'm sure Dad has forgiven you, Mom." And I was able to tell her in all honesty that I had forgiven her too. She was so close to death I could feel it hovering around her. I told my sister it wouldn't be long before she passed away. I didn't think she would live to see the spring.

The last time I saw Turkan, she was very frail and looked like a child in her bed. In her illness, she had developed a fixation for paper towels. She was convinced they were vital to her well-being, and she greatly feared she would run out of them. I went to the market, bought armloads of paper towels, and placed them around her bed.

"Look, Mother, you aren't going to run out of towels," I told her. "If you do, I will send money, and my sister will buy you more."

On my last night with her, I knew with surety I was not going to see her again, that this would be the last time. In the dark night, I sat on her bed and held her hand one last time in a final good-bye. We did not say much. She gently pulled me to lie on her chest, and she stroked my hair. I could hear her heartbeat. I felt no anger, no sorrow, no fear—only peace. The miracle of forgiveness had taken deep root in our souls.

* * *

During Mom's final days, I became very despondent. As she was dying, part of me was dying too. Saying good-bye to my dying mother from an ocean away was extremely difficult. I wanted to be there to hug her and tell her she was not alone, but I physically couldn't. I felt swamped with guilt and helplessness. The overwhelming feeling of inadequacy began to take its toll on my body and mind. I gradually lost my appetite and had difficulty sleeping, so much so that I became an insomniac and went down to one hundred and three pounds. Later I became paranoid of dying alone myself. The fear of loneliness was too much for me to handle.

After many days of internal battle, the depression once again won. I lost interest in all things. I actually wanted to disappear so I did not become a burden to anyone. Depression is like living with a rhinoceros lurking in the corner, quietly shifting its ponderous weight, ever present. You never know when it is going to raise its head and roll its terrible eyes. It is ready to charge and rend you with its merciless horn if it ever senses vulnerability. There is no defense; you are left quivering, torn, and bewildered. Then it retreats to bide its time until the next rush. You are always aware of its dark presence waiting for you in the shadows and wonder when it will charge again. Only someone who has gone through the experience can know what an immobilizing thing depression can be.

Since my son was on his mission at the time and my husband was working, I felt lonely, isolated, and unwanted. How grateful I am for good friends who lit up my dark world. Not only did they take care of me around the clock, but they also loved me more than I loved myself. Joanne McLeish would come every day to see me after she taught seminary, and I spent many days in her home. I remember sitting near her fireplace, praying and pleading with the Lord to take away some of the burden. On one hand, I was ready to be saved, and on the other hand, the great hollowness in my soul was killing me. I am truly grateful that the McLeishes never gave up on me or once complained. I received many blessings from Brother Steven Diaczun and my husband. The blessings were a great source of strength to me. I often felt I was carried in the arms of the Lord when I could not carry myself. With the great pain and agony I felt, Christ's Atonement took on a new meaning in my life. Once again, I sensed it was time to progress to a deeper level of understanding.

Turkan died on my birthday, April 8, 2008. When I heard she had died, I was actually relieved because she was no longer suffering. Her last days had been very challenging, and she had been very ill and weak from not eating. I couldn't get to the funeral; there wasn't time or money, and at the time of her death, I was ill myself. But I did pay for the funeral, and people commented on how nice it was, which is an important compliment in our culture. It brought honor to my family and helped me feel better about the whole situation. However, I admit I did not pay for a headstone. My father had not had one, and I wanted Turkan to disappear as completely as he had.

Cihangir had never visited her once in thirty-four years. I am sorry he did not get to know the relief and peace that come through reconciliation.

* * *

Turkan had always refused help for her illness. She would never admit that situations were beyond her control, and everything was always someone else's problem. I did not want to inherit that legacy from her. It took humility and courage to admit I needed professional help for my depression. I underwent counseling with LDS Social Services for a time to help me deal with the events in my childhood. All my life I'd had that vision of myself walking alone in the dark. My counselor, Bradley Miller, told me, "We'll work on it together, and someday in that darkness you will notice a street lamp, and then one day, it will eventually be daylight." He was right. Now when I think of that scene, it is filled with sunlight and flowers and children playing. It was a long, difficult journey from darkness to light, but it did eventually come. (Brother Miller also told me, "You and Moses have a lot in common. You are both basket cases.")

I enjoyed our talks. In fact, I looked forward to having chats with him. Week after week, my view of myself changed. In one of our sessions, he said something that really stuck with me. He told me that on the way to the Lord's mountain, some of us will have picnics and enjoy the scenery, while some of us will dangle from our climbing ropes. I felt I must be one of the ones constantly dangling, but at least I was given a good rope. And with help, I was also able to see the mountain, realize it was not insurmountable, and keep the goal in view.

Plowing the ground is painful. It tears up old beliefs, thought patterns, and habits by their roots. It leaves you torn, exposed, and hurting. But the plowing makes room for new growth, for whatever beautiful garden you choose to plant. You can choose to replace the hurtful things of your childhood with more beautiful, more useful things. I understand now that you can't have the growth without the plowing and the pain first. Though I still struggle with bouts of depression, and I will always bear the scars of my childhood, they no longer overly concern me. Instead, I focus on the garden, the beauty of my own choosing.

I have also learned the true power behind the principle of prayer. Quite simply, prayer works. Anytime I pray for something, it happens. My son will sometimes say to me, "This is a big one—you gotta pray for me." So I do, and it always works out. We have a standing joke in our house that if you have lost something you want back, just ask me to pray for it, and you will find it almost immediately. Seriously, though, I have learned in all sincerity to go to God with the smallest things because he always blesses His children with answers. He has indeed, with Christ, become my sanctuary and my solace.

Chapter Nineteen

"Live in thanksgiving daily, for the many mercies and blessings which [God] doth bestow upon you."
—Alma 34:38

I THINK THE TRIALS I have faced in my life have taught me to value human life more than anything. I know that everyone I meet has a story, and their stories are important. One human being can't be more of a human being than another—we're all equal. Everyone has a soul of great worth. And I love people because I love myself now. When people say they hurt, I don't compare pain anymore. I used to do that; I would think, "What do they know about pain? Mine is worse than anybody else's." But I don't feel the need to do that anymore. When someone complains about a problem, I no longer feel compelled to tell them about my own. I just listen to them. I look for signs in people to see if they're depressed and if anything can be done for them.

At times I think of the paths my life could have followed, and I marvel that I was rescued and brought to an understanding of the gospel and Christ's Atonement. I am filled with gratitude—not just for the life I have now but for the life I had then, which made me into the person I am now and brought me ultimately to where I stand today. Looking back, I can easily see the way the Lord's hand guided my life and how His grace attended me throughout the difficult times. I trust that it will continue to do so in whatever lies ahead. I have no illusions that the rest of my life, however long it may be, will be smooth sailing. That doesn't seem to be my trend. But I do feel better equipped and anchored to weather the storm.

I was once given this poem by a friend:

The anchor lifted, life adrift,
though white-capped seas may toss and shift,
despite the storm that surges now
and threatening spray against the bow,
the harbor's plotted, coordinates drawn
to sustain all until the dawn
reveals placid seas and gentle sky,
relief of spirit, tranquility.
To this we hold when all else goes—
the assurance of an anchored soul.

I didn't come to Canada for a "better life" like other immigrants might. I came simply because I loved my husband and couldn't imagine living without him. At the time of this writing, I have spent half my life in Turkey and half in Canada. I have gone through many changes— from Turkey to Canada, from Muslim to Mormon, and from adopted child to mother of an adopted child. I have gone from wealth to poverty and back again and am now in a fortunate position where I am happily able to share with others. Laughter comes easily to me now. No longer the injured child stealing to provide for myself alone, I want to help others in whatever way I can. I offer my story in the hope that it may do someone some good. If anything I have gone through allows me to be of help to someone else, then it has all been worthwhile.

And as always, I am launching into yet another new chapter of my life. John just recently married, and it was a temple wedding. And I just received a call from Church headquarters asking me to be involved in the translation of the Doctrine and Covenants into Turkish. We're off on another adventure!

A Note from Ross Hitchins

AYSE ESTABLISHED A GREAT FOUNDATION of love in our home. I could not have done half the things in the callings I've had without that foundation. Her actions indicate the strength of her testimony. As much as Ayse has learned about Western culture, I have learned about the gospel by watching her.

Her relationship with our son has been an inspiration to me. I don't think I really understood that until recently. I truly believe the goodness with which God blessed our son was magnified by what his mother taught him and also by her example to him throughout the years. As John said, she knows what she's talking about, and she means what she says. Because of Ayse, I have a *huge* testimony of mothers. I am grateful and honored to be her husband.

—Ross

Top row: Fatma's half brother Millic holding his daughter Ayse and Mustafa with Cihangir (prior to Cihangir being adopted by Turkan and Necmi). Bottom row: Mustafa's mother, Havva; Fatma's mother, Hatice, holding Mustafa; Fatma holding Hatice; Mehmet.

Turkan (left) and Ayse (right).

The judge and his wife.

From left: Ayse, Necmi, and Cihangir.

Turkan (left) and Necmi (right).

Ayse at her university graduation.

From left: Fatma, Asye, and Turkan.

Ayse in Cukurbag at the house where she was born.

From left: Ayse; her mother, Fatma; and Fatma's mother, Hatice.

Ayse in Cukurbag.

Cukurbag.

From left: Ross, Stephanie, John, and Ayse.

About the Author

AYSE HITCHINS IS A CITIZEN of the world and recognizes no boundaries or limitations. She now lives in Canada with her family but will be returning to her native land of Turkey soon. Her life has been one giant roller coaster, from one extreme to the other, and she's still enjoying the ride. In many ways, she has experienced enough to fill two lifetimes. Ayse loves education and has graduated from college twice with degrees in music and sociology. Ayse's mother was adopted, so was Ayse, and she has raised an adopted child. Her favorite hobbies are her husband and her son.